LARSTAN'S THE BLACK BOOK™ ON GOVERNMENT SECURITY

by Gregory N. Akers, Doron Cohen & Robert J. Worner,
Mary Ann Davidson, Dr. Alastair MacWillson & Eric Stange,
Paul B. Patrick, Jim Porell, Donald A. "Andy" Purdy, Jr., S. Rao Vasireddy

Published by:
Larstan Publishing Inc.
10604 Outpost Dr., N. Potomac, MD 20878
240-396-0007 ext. 901
www.larstan.com

PRINTED IN THE UNITED STATES OF AMERICA

Design by Rob Hudgins & 5050Design.com
ISBN, Print Edition 978-0-9764266-3-9
Library of Congress Control Number: 2006924521
First Edition

LARSTAN's THE BLACK BOOK™ ON

GOVERNMENT SECURITY

ADVANCED GOVERNMENT SECURITY STRATEGIES FROM THE INDUSTRY'S PREMIERE THOUGHT LEADERS

Gregory N. Akers ■
Doron Cohen & Robert J. Worner ■
Mary Ann Davidson ■
Dr. Alastair MacWillson & Eric Stange ■
Paul B. Patrick ■
Jim Porell ■
Donald A. "Andy" Purdy, Jr. ■
S. Rao Vasireddy ■

LARSTAN
PUBLISHING

WASHINGTON D.C. ■ PHILADELPHIA

TABLE OF CONTENTS

DEDICATIONS

To the men and women of the National Cyber Security Division and the United States Computer Emergency Readiness Team (US-CERT) who continue to inspire me with their tireless efforts to enhance our nation's cyber preparedness. To those in government and industry who dedicate their time and expertise to address the cyber security challenge. To my wife, Robin, and daughter, Alexandra, whose love, support, and encouragement is exemplified in everything I do. — *Donald A. "Andy" Purdy, Jr.*

I dedicate my chapter to my wife, Cathy, and my children, Suzanne and Kevin. I would also like to thank the tremendously talented engineers, systems administrators and managers of Cisco Systems for the truly unique environment that they have allowed me to engage in for more than a decade. — *Greg Akers*

I dedicate my chapter to the United States Department of Defense. Everything I learned about leadership I learned while serving in the U.S. Navy. What inspires me to be more and to do more are the lessons of military history and the sacrifices of those who served this country in war and in peace. Bless them all. Si vis pacem, para bellum: If you want peace, prepare for the war. (Vegetius) — *Mary Ann Davidson*

I would like to thank my colleagues at Bell Laboratories and Lucent Technologies, whose efforts were critical in developing the Bell Labs security model that is instrumental in driving the ITU-T X.805 / ISO 18028-2 standards, which are also the basis for this paper. I am grateful to the invaluable help from Suhasini Sabnis, Uma Chandrashekhar, Adrian Hartman and Kathleen Cowles for reviewing the content and for encouraging me to tackle this complex subject. I also appreciate all the efforts of Eric Green, David Evancha and John Persinos at the Larstan Publishing for making this project a success — *S. Rao Vasireddy*

I dedicate my chapter to my wife, Anat, and my children, Raz and Shaked, for their love and support that inspires me every day. Many thanks to all my colleagues at BMC Software for their dedication, professionalism and vision in creating Identity Management solutions. Special thanks to Rami Elron for his insight, comments and guidance throughout this project and to Cindy Sterling for her incredible support and enthusiasm in making this chapter a reality. — *Doron Cohen*

I dedicate this chapter to my wife, Beth, and my two sons, Matt and Adam, who provide the incredible support and love that keeps me going and to my father for showing me the definition of great engineering. A special thanks to Cindy Sterling for her constant contributions and drive to make this chapter happen. Finally, many thanks to all my co-workers over the last decade for always being willing to push the envelope in order to achieve truly great things. — *Bob Worner*

I dedicate this to all of my colleagues in Accenture who have worked with me over the past three years to set a new standard of excellence in global information security services. —*Alastair MacWillson*

I dedicate this to the Accenture Homeland Security team that practices in this realm on a daily basis. I appreciate their assistance in completing this project. — *Eric S. Stange*

To my children and parents, for their encouragement and patience as we all grow older and attempt to act younger. And to my friends and colleagues at IBM that offer support and wonderful ideas toward the next generation of enterprise computing. — *Jim Porell*

I dedicate this work to my mother and father who provided the encouragement and support in my many endeavors, to my wife and kids who have been there for me even when I was gone so much on business and all the members of the BEA federal team who work tirelessly to ensure that I understand the special requirements of the systems used to protect this great country. — *Paul B. Patrick*

THE TEAM

Editorial Director | John Persinos
Managing Editor | David Evancha
Contributing Editor | Jonathan Holasek
Creative Director | Rob Hudgins

Group Publisher | Eric S. Green
Editorial Advisory Board | Robert L. Bush, Jacob Goodwin, Howard A. Schmidt, Edward Tyler
COO | Stan Genkin
CEO | Larry Genkin

FOREWORD

By Howard A. Schmidt

When it comes to cyber security, the private and public sectors share many similarities. An IT system is an IT system, regardless of the organization. Data management lessons learned in the private sector, and those learned in the government sector, are quite alike. How they differ are the products and services produced and their overall impact on society.

A computer virus that invades a large company may cause email to slow down, quarterly or annual financials to get misquoted or improper billing in shipping. To be sure, all pose major problems, but at the end of the day, they only affect that particular company and its customers. The costs are usually tallied in dollars and cents. The stakes are considerably higher for government agencies. Public safety and national security often hangs in the balance, with the costs counted in human lives.

For example, if that same virus affected a public 911 system based on Voice over IP (VoIP) that needed to communicate to a backend database, urgent 911 calls might not get through, depriving the emergency system of its ability to dispatch calls, except through radio and other media that most people are no longer accustomed to relying on during emergencies.

This virus can impede one company's ability to efficiently conduct business or a city's ability to respond to an emergency. The systems and viruses may be the same, but the results are very different. If an organization's "product" is national security or public safety, the consequences of a cyber breach are dramatic and widespread, on a municipal, state or national level. This assertion does not, by any means, intend to discount the consequences in the private sector, where jobs, health benefits, retirement plans and personal finances can take a big hit. But attacks on the integrity and security of data in the public sector can adversely impact millions of lives and the entire commonweal.

In addition to the different ramifications of systems failures, the other public-private distinction in the security realm is the source of funding that's invested in IT systems. During the early days of government IT, the National Security Agency (NSA) or the U.S. Department of Defense (DoD) mandated security preparedness. A government agency was compelled to petition the NSA to buy security technology, which in turn was developed on a custom basis for government use. However, federal managers soon realized that it was cheaper to buy Commercial Off-The-Shelf Technology (COTS), because private companies were producing more innovative products faster and at lower costs.

This early distinction between government-developed software and COTS is the primary reason why government IT practices can be different from those in the private sector. I once asked the former Chief of Staff of the U.S. Air Force, "How was the decision made to transition from closed, off-the-net government systems over to the Internet and the use of those protocols that we use today?" His answer was simple: "It was more cost effective." The government can get the same benefits at much less cost.

Today, government IT managers are working hard to emulate their private sector counterparts, by embracing innovation and efficiency. Government wants email, transaction processing, international communications and continual modernization. The government's old approach to technology is analogous to when the military would, say, build a specific-use pickup truck at an extremely high unit cost, merely to transport people and material, when a conventional Ford or General Motors truck from the assembly line would have done the job just as well.

Also emerging is a higher level of oversight on spending for public IT systems. These costs tend to be more closely scrutinized by the agencies themselves, and through "report cards" sent directly to Congress. Of course, there always will exist specification requirements that preclude most civilian companies from making certain military equipment, such as tanks or jet fighters. However, this obstacle does not exist within IT, where the commercial sector performs best. As a large procurer and user of commercial IT products, the government has an increasing stake in the efficacy and security of private hardware and software companies.

INTRODUCTION

By William F. Pelgrin

Ronald Reagan once famously said: "The nine most terrifying words in the English language are, 'I'm from the government and I'm here to help.'"

Inside the government itself, the most terrifying words in the English language may be: "The information security office is here to facilitate your office's goals and objectives." The book you now hold in your hands is designed to alleviate that terror.

The Black Book on Government Security was written to help managers and information security professionals understand the key cyber security challenges faced by all levels of government. This book will explore many of the issues involved and provide concrete guidelines for implementing sound security practices.

The fact is, information security was often perceived as an impediment — as added cost and time. For the most part, it was an afterthought, if it was thought of at all. This perception that information security is an obstacle to getting things done is changing. More than ever, all levels of government are becoming aware of the importance of cyber security.

However, awareness is one thing; action is another. One of government's biggest challenges is to transition from a general awareness of cyber security to concrete implementation of good cyber security practices.

How does government ensure that cyber security issues are championed by leadership, embraced by business managers, implemented by users and understood by all? Getting it done can be like herding cats, especially when cyber threats are very difficult to understand. A cyber attack is so amorphous it is often difficult to grasp the concept. It's nearly impossible to determine where a cyber attack will come from, who will launch it, the exact target and the nature and extent of the payload.

This uncertainty is fostering an accelerating loss of trust in the systems we have relied on for years. Can we trust that the technology will be there when needed, and that the entity we're communicating with is actually what we think it is? Technology itself is posing the danger, as concerns grow over phishing, data theft, spamming, spoofing and other malicious activities that negatively affect the efficiency and effectiveness of day-to-day business. Once seen as a "silver bullet" to solve a multitude of problems, computer technology is increasingly under attack. Thousands of new vulnerabilities and corresponding worms and viruses are reported each year.

Government now has a unique opportunity to establish information security as an enabler, to help return the value of technology to the business process.

Security can no longer be an afterthought. The threats are real and the cost of insecurity too great. State governments over the last few years have made progress in improving their overall cyber security posture, but there is still a lot to accomplish. Notably, there is concern that the latest security improvements will have a short shelf life. To continue its progress on the security front, the public sector must permanently transform individual attitudes and organizational culture, no matter how daunting this transformation appears.

THE TENETS FOR SUCCESS

Government must recognize the changing security landscape and adjust its efforts accordingly. Understanding and implementing the following tenets are ingredients for success, to help ensure that government is as cyber-secure as possible:

- Cyber security is everyone's responsibility. Everyone from the executive to the end user must understand his or her respective roles and responsibilities regarding cyber security.
- A commitment to the importance of cyber security is accomplished one step at a time. Chunk it up into manageable goals. Be very deliverable-oriented. And remember, it is the start that stops most people.

- Cyber security officers must communicate in a way that is visual, tangible and actionable. Make it real for those who need to hear the message.
- Sound, good security practices must be second nature — just like buckling a seat belt.
- Outreach and education efforts are essential to raise the necessary awareness level if we are to be as prepared as possible.
- Government leadership must be proactive in the cyber security arena and work hard to ensure that each of us understands the important role we play in securing cyber space.
- Protecting the critical assets with which the government is entrusted is one of government's top priorities. Government information, in such areas as Social Security, health care and taxes — is sensitive and confidential. Under many circumstances, there is a legal obligation to keep that information private and secure. It is incumbent on government officials to understand how to protect data and monitor its controls. Appropriate policies must be in place, to understand where vulnerabilities exist and make informed decisions about security network investments.

More than 10,000 new computer viruses were reported in 2004; it now only takes a few minutes to compromise an unprotected computer that is connected to the Internet. The negative impact of a virus or computer compromise can be devastating on networks, on the information contained within those systems and, just as important, on the confidence of those who trust government for protection.

- Government must break down the code of silence. "If you don't know, it really didn't happen," is an unacceptable attitude, and it must be changed. We must share information; thankfully, this is beginning to happen. We must also understand the importance of working together as a team in a collaborative and cooperative manner, to address cyber security issues. Government managers must create an environment that encourages collaboration. The culture can't be about blame, or we all lose. A paramount value must be learning from the past, to improve the future.

■ We cannot do this alone. Because the cyber realm knows no geographic boundaries, managers and security professionals must work closely with government entities at all levels. One such collaborative mechanism is the Multi-State Information Sharing and Analysis Center (MS-ISAC). The MS-ISAC fosters collaboration and knowledge sharing among, and between, the states. By having these strong partnerships, we can be better prepared collectively. Again, the theme is collaboration.

Two key words should be government's slogan in the fight against cyber attacks — vigilance and resilience.

■ Vigilance, because achieving 100 percent security is unobtainable. Good security is never one layer deep; it consists of multiple layers. Cyber security is akin to physical security, in that constant work is necessary for protection.

■ Resilience, because it is not whether you get knocked down, but how quickly and securely you can get back up.

When there is a crisis — when everything else is failing — citizens look to government for stability, protection and leadership. Government can't fail its citizens.

To effect genuine, far-reaching change, there must be a fundamental culture shift. Cyber security is not the sole purview of technologists. Security and critical infrastructure protection also entail awareness of vulnerabilities and risks; as such, everyone involved shares the responsibility of taking prudent and proactive measures. By working collaboratively, we all can play important roles in ensuring vigilance and resilience.

Traditionally, the issues of security, especially cyber security, have not been integral parts of our daily lives. However, as society faces new and constantly evolving threats, security awareness and practices must be second nature. *The Black Book on Government Security* is designed to help its readers become ardent champions of enhanced cyber security. By following the advice and practices conveyed within these pages, you will be better prepared to set an example for, and change the culture of, your own organization.

[1]

IMPLEMENTING A NATIONAL CYBER SECURITY STRATEGY

In the face of growing threats to its cyber assets, America requires the coordinated implementation of a cohesive and comprehensive plan to protect its vital and most sensitive data. Here, one of the leading decision makers in the federal government IT arena conveys how the federal government is working with public and private stakeholders to implement the overarching priorities for securing the country's cyberspace.

> "THE SUPERIOR MAN, WHEN RESTING IN SAFETY, DOES NOT FORGET THAT DANGER MAY COME. WHEN IN A STATE OF SECURITY HE DOES NOT FORGET THE POSSIBILITY OF RUIN. WHEN ALL IS ORDERLY, HE DOES NOT FORGET THAT DISORDER MAY COME."
> — Confucius

by DONALD A. "ANDY" PURDY, JR.

In today's world, the traditional security paradigm is shifting to encompass the unique challenges presented by the digital landscape. Information Technology (IT) and the cyber infrastructure are critical to our economy, our homeland security, our law enforcement and public safety and our privacy. Cyber systems support everything from food distribution to financial transactions to national security. This reliance on cyber systems extends across the public sector, the private sector and to individual citizens.

The cyber infrastructure has no boundaries, and threats often do not conform to traditional models. Due to our increasing dependency on cyber systems, the consequences of a successful cyber attack on individuals, businesses and federal agencies could have a devastating effect on our nation. The Department of Homeland Security believes that the implementation of a risk management approach to assess risk, prioritize resources and execute protective measures is critical to securing our nation, including our cyber infrastructure.

The National Cyber Security Division (NCSD) of Homeland Security applies this risk management approach to the cyber component of the Preparedness mission. The mission of NCSD is to work collaboratively with public, private and international entities to secure cyberspace and America's cyber assets.

This chapter will review how NCSD meets its mission by applying a risk management approach through two strategic priorities:
❶ to build an effective national cyber security response system, and
❷ to implement a cyber risk management program for critical infrastructure protection.

But government does not do this alone. Partnerships and collaboration across government at all levels and with the private sector, both domestically and internationally, are the keys to determining the requirements and scope of both of these priorities, and for effective implementation as well. This process will help the department, and the nation as a whole, to effectively focus the appropriate roles and necessary resources on the most pressing risks.

Finally, we will discuss how information sharing and analysis, the foundation of our ability to respond to an incident, can be improved.

GOVERNMENT ROLE IN PROTECTING AMERICA'S CYBERSPACE

Security is a shared societal responsibility. As the owners of more than 85 percent of the national physical and cyber infrastructure assets, the private sector and the general public are key partners in successful infrastructure protection. Each person and organization that is involved with computers, information systems, the Internet or wireless devices must be aware of the importance of cyber security and its interconnected nature. The private sector is the driving force for developing new software to defend against cyber attacks and to develop more secure software. As the primary owners of the cyber infrastructure assets, as well as infrastructure assets that rely on cyber systems, the private sector has a vested interest in keeping one step ahead of cyber threats by appropriately mitigating their cyber risks.

The government has a key role to play in cyber security. Across the federal, state and local government this role encompasses five specific aspects of cyber security:

❶ consumer protection/cyber fraud prevention provided by the Federal Trade Commission,

❷ law enforcement and intelligence provided by the Federal Bureau of Investigation (FBI) and the U.S. Secret Service,

❸ information security standards and guidelines provided by the National Institute of Standards and Technology (NIST),

❹ information sharing throughout state and local governments coordinated by the Multi-State Information Sharing and Analysis Center (MS-ISAC), and

❺ cyber preparedness/cyber infrastructure response, recovery and protection coordinated by the NCSD of the Department of Homeland Security. These interconnected relationships formalize the traditional law enforcement and risk management approaches and can be seen in Figure 1.

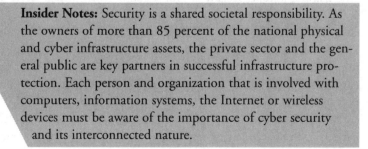

Insider Notes: Security is a shared societal responsibility. As the owners of more than 85 percent of the national physical and cyber infrastructure assets, the private sector and the general public are key partners in successful infrastructure protection. Each person and organization that is involved with computers, information systems, the Internet or wireless devices must be aware of the importance of cyber security and its interconnected nature.

FIGURE 1 - GOVERNMENT'S ROLE IN CYBER SECURITY

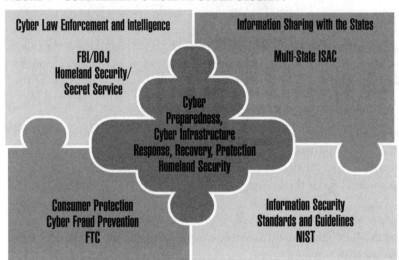

These relationships cover the spectrum of cyber security needs from the preparedness and, importantly, the empowerment of individual consumers, to the protection of the digital control systems of critical infrastructures, to the investigation and prosecution of the cyber criminals responsible for attacks or thefts. These relationships are interwoven, as each agency acts as the focal point for their area of expertise, and each partner closely with other agencies and the private sector.

In addition to these roles, government has the vital responsibility to protect both the information and infrastructure of our citizens. Focusing on securing the government systems that contain this essential information is of key importance, especially at Homeland Security, which serves as a focal point for securing government's cyberspace.

Homeland Security created the National Cyber Security Division (NCSD) to provide the federal government with a centralized cyber security coordination and preparedness function. Based on the *National Strategy to Secure Cyberspace* and Homeland Security Presidential Directive (HSPD)-7, NCSD has identified two overarching priorities: 1) to build an effective national cyberspace security response system, and 2) to implement a cyber risk management program for critical infrastructure protection. Focusing on these two priorities establishes the framework for securing cyberspace today and lays a foundation for addressing future cyber issues and threats.

PRIORITY ONE: BUILDING A NATIONAL CYBERSPACE SECURITY RESPONSE SYSTEM

The first priority of the *National Strategy to Secure Cyberspace* is the creation and maintenance of a National Cyberspace Security Response System. As implemented by NCSD, the System brings together the coordinating leadership, processes and protocols that will determine when and what actions to be taken to protect the critical cyber infrastructure. Such a system requires public and private collaboration on a number of different components, including situational awareness, analysis, response and recovery.

Homeland Security leads public sector collaboration, in partnership with the Executive Office of the President, the Departments of Justice and Defense and other federal agencies. In coordination with the Department of State and other federal agencies, the government is also working to facilitate and leverage related capabilities on a global basis.

SITUATIONAL AWARENESS

Situational awareness is the starting point of the Response System. The initial objective in creating this system has been to build a robust, cyber situational awareness capability that creates the ability to detect and recognize cyber incidents and activity of significance to governments or the critical infrastructure, in tandem with information sharing among government departments, and between the government and the private sector. This requires a strong partnership and collaborative effort between governments at all levels, both domestic and international, and between governments and the private sector on a worldwide basis.

Situational awareness efforts create the ability to detect and recognize significant or anomalous cyber activity from among the abundance of the "white noise" that is normal cyberspace activity. Data flow into this process is critical to understanding the true current status of the cyber infrastructure and must come from public and private entities across the critical infrastructure sectors.

The U.S. Computer Emergency Readiness Team (US-CERT) Operations Center is NCSD's 24x7x365 watch and warning capability and analysis center. US-CERT is the key operational mechanism for sharing cyber security information with the nation, coordinating incident response activities, providing situational awareness and analyzing incidents and malicious code.

NCSD created US-CERT in September 2003 to protect the nation's Internet infrastructure by coordinating defense against and response to cyber attacks. It is a focal point in information sharing and collaboration with federal agencies, the private sector, the research community, state and local governments and international entities. The team also regularly collaborates with domestic and international computer security incident response teams. Significantly, US-CERT has become a trusted third-party to assist in the responsible handling and disclosure of vulnerabilities. A high level view of the multitude of information sharing sources is seen in figure 2.

FIGURE 2 - INFORMATION SHARING SOURCES

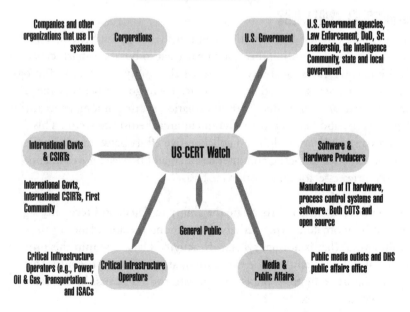

US-CERT Information Workflow

As the government works to ensure the consistent and timely sharing of information within government, communication and collaboration toward building situational awareness becomes of utmost importance. In partnership with the Office of Management and Budget (OMB), NCSD, as the leader of US-CERT, has issued the US-CERT Federal Concept of Operations (CONOPs) that maps to the Federal Information Security Management Act's (FISMA) requirement for civilian agencies to report cyber incidents to US-CERT. Agencies are required to report to US-CERT and OMB important cyber incidents and information.

US-CERT is attempting to leverage the information flows and capabilities of federal government agencies along with the Department of Defense, civilian agencies, the Intelligence community and law enforcement. By undertaking the considerable challenge of discerning what is significant among all the data passing through the Internet, Homeland Security is trying to build a common picture of Internet health in general, and of key government and critical infrastructure systems in particular. US-CERT's Situational Awareness Program and Internet Health and Status service is used by 50 government agency computer security incident response teams.

ANALYSIS
After analyzing incidents reported by these entities and coordinating with national security incident response centers responding to incidents on both classified and unclassified systems, US-CERT assesses the potential cyber threats.

US-CERT identifies and analyzes malicious code, correlates incident data from a myriad of disparate reporting sources and supports ongoing federal law enforcement investigations through computer forensics and information exchange. Other malicious activities include: worms, viruses and their variants, significant malicious criminal or targeted cyber attack activity, the unexplained failures of key systems and the discovery of new vulnerabilities and active exploits. As an increasingly trusted third party, US-CERT confers closely with developers in the private sector to analyze and manage vulnerabilities.

GIVEN TODAY'S HIGHLY INTERCONNECTED ENVIRONMENT, A COMMON APPROACH IS REQUIRED TO UNIFY THE PROTECTIVE ACTIVITIES WITHIN PUBLIC, PRIVATE AND INTERNATIONAL ENTITIES, AND SECURE CYBER INFRASTRUCTURE.

US-CERT also runs a robust Malware Lab that provides behavior techniques for dynamic and static analysis, reviews malicious code for "novel" attacks (those that are unknown to date), supports forensic investigations with cursive analysis on artifacts and provides on-site malware analytic and recovery support.

RESPONSE

Having a clear understanding of the situation enables the government to act appropriately and expeditiously as incidents arise. The results of US-CERT's analyses are communicated externally in an actionable manner through established relationships and protocols, throughout the federal government and with the general population of computer users. These reports allow for a proportionate response that can escalate as necessary.

The NCSD is part of the Preparedness Directorate at Homeland Security. The Directorate is responsible for preparing Americans to respond to incidents and disasters through developing and improving the appropriate coordination protocols. Homeland Security is constantly working to enhance its preparedness in order to respond to serious malicious activities and to reduce cyber vulnerabilities. This effort spans government-wide preparedness and that of the privately owned critical infrastructure. A key function of this response effort is to work with the private sector on response actions and alert stakeholders about our analysis and recommended actions.

The capability to provide alerts and warnings to the government and the private sector is, in itself, a critical component of a national cyberspace security response system. Alerts from the private sector are supplemented by government alerts issued through the National Cyber Alert System, maintained by US-CERT.

The National Cyber Alert System disseminates reasoned and actionable cyber security information to the public based on US-CERT analysis and situational awareness efforts. These Alerts may be technical guidance to reduce specific vulnerabilities or "non-technical" step by step actions to protect against an immediate cyber threat. Among the malicious activities that would trigger a response are worms, viruses and their variants, significant malicious criminal or targeted cyber attack activity, unexplained failures of key systems and the discovery of new vulnerabilities and active exploits.

Timely and actionable alerts and warnings are communicated to government departments, Internet Service Providers (ISPs), managed service providers, network operators and private system owners and operators so they can take protective action on their systems and those of their customers. This helps to prevent potentially serious problems from spreading throughout the Internet with cascading consequences to the critical infrastructures and our citizens.

Alerts and situational reports are delivered to the Homeland Security Operations Center (HSOC). The HSOC adds this constant flow of analyzed data to its analysis of the overall Homeland situational awareness to continue to "connect the dots" and determine what response is needed. US-CERT and the HSOC work closely together on everyday incidents and serious incidents that may have a significant impact on critical infrastructures or federal systems and will escalate the issue as needed.

Insider Notes: Examples of cyber emergencies that trigger government responses include: confirmed significant cyber incident/attacks directed at one or more national critical infrastructures; cyber incidents impacting or potentially impacting national security, or having a substantial impact on national economic security, public health or safety, or public confidence and morale; discovery of an exploitable vulnerability in a widely used protocol; or other complex or unusual circumstances related to a cyber incident requiring interagency coordination.

HOMELAND SECURITY IS FOCUSED ON RAISING CYBER SECURITY AWARENESS LEVELS AND DISSEMINATING TIMELY AND ACTIONABLE INFORMATION TO THE PUBLIC, PRIVATE SECTOR AND INTERNATIONAL STAKEHOLDERS.

In the event of a cyber Incident of National Significance, the National Cyber Response Coordination Group (NCRCG) will help to coordinate the federal response, including law enforcement and the intelligence community, with that of the private sector. This forum facilitates coordination of intra-governmental and public-private preparedness and operations to respond to, and recover from, incidents and attacks that have significant cyber consequences.

The NCRCG is a forum of 13 principal agencies coordinating intra-governmental and public-private preparedness and operations. NCRCG brings together senior officials from national security, law enforcement, defense, intelligence and other government agencies that maintain significant cyber security responsibilities and capabilities. Under Homeland Security, NCSD is the executive agent for the NCRCG, and the NCRCG co-chairs are Homeland Security, the Department of Defense and the Department of Justice.

While the NCRCG regularly monitors cyber threat activity, it is officially activated during a cyber incident that may relate to or constitute terrorist attack, terrorist threat, threat to national security, disaster or any other cyber emergency requiring federal government response. Examples of cyber emergencies that trigger government responses include: confirmed significant cyber incident/attacks directed at one or more national critical infrastructures; cyber incidents impacting or potentially impacting national security, or having a substantial impact on national economic security, public health or safety, or public confidence and morale; discovery of an exploitable vulnerability in a widely used protocol; or other complex or unusual circumstances related to a cyber incident requiring interagency coordination.

The NCRCG addresses both sudden incidents of limited duration and gradually escalating cyber threats and crises. As referenced in National Response Plan's (NRP) Cyber Incident Annex, the NCRCG supports the Inter-agency Incident Management Group (IIMG), member-agency department heads and the Executive Office of the President (EOP), as appropriate, in regard to cyber-related issues. These efforts, along with exercises to test and train their use, are advancing preparedness by systematizing our response mechanisms and actions.

Homeland Security is working to extend this coordinated preparedness to the private sector so it is clear how the government and the private sector will coordinate the response to a cyber incident of national significance, such as a cyber attack or the cyber consequences of a natural disaster or physical attack. The private sector is well prepared for the typical kinds of attacks it sees every day. However, it is essential to enhance coordinated preparedness to respond to the most serious types of attacks, which have already been experienced or can be imagined, that pose great risk to our government and critical infrastructure.

RECOVERY

There are a number of aspects to the recovery process in the case of a cyber incident. For example, based on the need, US-CERT provides on-site incident response and recovery capabilities to federal agencies and to other systems that might have a detrimental affect on federal or critical infrastructures. Analysts tailor their recovery support as needed and help begin the rebuilding process through reducing vulnerabilities and preparing for future incidents impacting these critical systems.

Recovery efforts are also supplemented by active coordination with law enforcement agencies. US-CERT Operations actively supports ongoing law enforcement investigations by providing key information for case files. This information is the basis for locating and arresting perpetrators of the cyber incident. US-CERT also supports forensic investigations with recursive analysis on artifacts.

Planning for recovery on a national level is a complex issue. Homeland Security is actively incorporating the lessons from Hurricanes Katrina and

Rita and other incidents into recovery plans for the future. The effort has focused agency attention on learning the cyber impact of widespread disasters, be they natural or caused by terrorism. On a basic level, this includes the need to back up systems (with ongoing integrity safeguards) and to have business continuity/disaster recovery plans in place in anticipation of major disruptions. With the increasing dependence on cyber resources, it is essential that private networks and enterprises and government agencies plan effectively for what they will do to restore services after a disruption.

The NRP provides recovery direction on a number of different subject areas. It addresses cyber Incidents of National Significance in fairly broad terms within the Cyber Annex. The roles of government and the private sector are laid out in very general terms, but subsequent work on the NCRCG protocols are adding increased granularity and clarity to who will do what during a nationally significant cyber incident.

The NRP also includes a formal series of resources provided by the federal government, which are grouped into 12 Emergency Support Functions (ESF). The communications component is led by NCSD's counterpart organization for telecommunications, the National Communications System (NCS). ESF-2 encompasses recovery from communications disruptions caused by natural disasters or attacks of any kind. Although the NCS has significant experience working with the private sector to facilitate recovery of critical communications functions, further consideration is being given to whether the IT portion of communications is adequately covered in the ESF-2 and whether standard operating procedures (SOPs) are necessary to more comprehensively address IT issues. Questions may also be raised about whether IT disruptions affecting the private sector are appropriately and adequately covered in the current scope of the ESF-2.

To address a specific need in recovery efforts in the immediate aftermath of an incident, Homeland Security is seeking to establish an initiative to implement the "NET Guard" provision of the Homeland Security Act of 2002. The provision, proposed by Senator Wyden (D-OR) and Senator Allen (R-VA), calls for the establishment of a national technology guard, to be known as "NET Guard", comprised of local teams of volunteers with expertise in relevant areas of science and technology, to assist local communities to respond and recover from attacks on information systems and communications networks.

There have been numerous accounts from recent experiences about both the need for specific technical assistance/resources immediately following the incident and the private sector's desire and ability to help address that need. There have also been accounts about the inability to match needs with available resources in a timely fashion and the federal government's challenges in providing assistance in this process. Homeland Security recognizes the importance of the role such a program could play in responding to and recovering from a potential disaster and supports working collaboratively with private sector partners to improve response and recovery efforts.

One area for consideration in the context of this initiative is whether during a significant disruption there is a need for a clearinghouse for IT requirements. If a disruption occurs, such a capability could assist in the recovery effort by facilitating the articulation of requirements in a way that is meaningful and searchable, and then quickly matching them with entities that can meet those requirements.

The second capability under development is whether there needs to be pre-cleared volunteer teams of IT professionals who, for a brief period of time, can be brought into an area suffering a major disruption to help restore critical systems. The thinking is that after a disruption, even if all necessary equipment is provided and delivered to the affected area, experts will be needed and will require appropriate access to help get the systems back up and running rapidly and effectively.

Insider Notes: Locally grown volunteer teams can be pre-cleared to help in areas that face major disruptions that are too big a task for their own locally grown teams, such as the Gulf region after a hurricane. The area that is recovering from a disaster can report that they have certain requirements and require specific assistance and these needs could then be matched up with the pre-cleared teams around the country, who could then be brought into the area for a short-term, SWAT-like effort to help get systems back up and running.

These volunteer teams will bring to bear specific expertise and can help address requirements, such as the need for backup power for communications. These teams could be called on when other communities need assistance in a crisis. Locally grown volunteer teams can be pre-cleared to help in areas that face major disruptions that are too big a task for their own locally grown teams, such as the Gulf region after a hurricane. The area that is recovering from a disaster can report that they have certain requirements and require specific assistance and these needs could then be matched up with the pre-cleared teams around the country, who could then be brought into the area for a short-term, SWAT-like effort to help get systems back up and running.

Part of the exploration of the issues will be whether there is or should be a regional, local or community-based approach to recovery that can do the requisite advanced planning necessary to expedite recovery. Pursuit of these answers involves partnership with a number of DHS components and outreach to state, local and private sector entities to explore the possibility of creating locally organized groups to prepare for these immediate recovery activities.

INTERNATIONAL EFFORTS

The *National Strategy to Secure Cyberspace* recognized that international cooperation is crucial to helping to secure our national cyberspace. International cooperation in cyber security helps to foster national and international activities that promote a culture of security and improve the Nation's overall incident preparedness and response posture. Because of the global nature of cyberspace, international cooperation and collaborative action are imperative to building the relationships needed to prevent, predict, detect, respond to and reconstitute rapidly after cyber incidents. Based on its mission to implement the Strategy, NCSD has incorporated collaboration with international entities into an International Program toward its goals to establish a national cyber security response system and reduce cyber vulnerabilities.

Specifically, a three-part strategy guides NCSD's international engagement in accordance with the overall mission of securing national cyberspace. The strategy includes the following elements:

- Engage in international outreach activities to build awareness about the global cyber risk, to share information about the role and activities of computer security incident response teams to mitigate the risk and to build relationships among governments toward global cooperation on cyber security.
- Establish information sharing relationships, communications mechanisms and collaborative arrangements to increase our global cyber situational awareness; leverage global expertise; share best practices, experiences and specific threat and vulnerability information; and coordinate global cyber incident response.
- Establish collaborative arrangements for addressing the cyber component of critical infrastructure protection issues.

NCSD is working strategically with key allies on cyber security policy and operational cooperation. Leveraging pre-existing relationships among Computer Security Incident Response Teams (CSIRTs), NCSD has established a preliminary framework for cooperation on cyber security policy, watch warning and incident response with key allies, Australia, Canada, New Zealand and the United Kingdom. Additionally, the framework incorporates efforts on key strategic issues as agreed upon by these allies.

NCSD is also coordinating and participating in the establishment of an International Watch and Warning Network (IWWN) among cyber security policy, computer emergency response and law enforcement representa-

Insider Notes: The regular sharing of information will help establish trust relationships that are vital to ensure information flow in the event of a major cyber incident. By putting more effort into establishing trust relationships and communications mechanisms, it may be possible to accelerate the enhancement of global cyber situational awareness. One of the major challenges to these efforts is to establish a system whereby countries can share raw information that provides value to their individual efforts.

tives. In October 2004, the United States and Germany cosponsored a 15-nation international cyber security conference in Berlin. This event included a tabletop exercise to both explore communication paths and processes and to build an international watch and warning network to help participating nations enhance their cyber situational awareness. Following the conference, a working group was formed that included representatives from the 15 countries. An initial priority was to leverage global regional models of information sharing and enhance efforts to encourage trusted relationships of sharing. Once it is implemented, the IWWN will provide a mechanism for the participating countries to share information to build global cyber situational awareness and coordinate incident response.

As efforts are undertaken, such as those with our allies and the IWWN, to build global cyber situational awareness and share information on watch, warning and incident response, the question of exactly what type of information should be shared and when will need to be addressed. It is notable that much of the international dialogue surrounding information sharing is concentrated on processes and mechanisms for sharing sensitive information such as new vulnerabilities. While that information is important, it is also necessary to expend resources on parallel efforts to facilitate the regular sharing of non-sensitive information and analysis among the international community.

The regular sharing of information will help establish trust relationships that are vital to ensure information flow in the event of a major cyber incident. By putting more effort into establishing trust relationships and communications mechanisms, it may be possible to accelerate the enhancement of global cyber situational awareness. One of the major challenges to these efforts is to establish a system whereby countries can share raw information that provides value to their individual efforts.

For example, at one point during the course of the table top exercise during the Berlin conference, one country representative asked how to determine when to share a particular piece of information. When does anomalous information, an incident or a vulnerability, rise to the level of significance that it needs to be shared internationally? The consensus answer was that if one waits until an individual piece of information in an individual country has attained international significance before sharing it, it might be too late to take appropriate measures before there are serious consequences. This reinforces the importance of regularized information sharing among countries. It also emphasizes the need to ultimately establish a balance between sharing everything, trying to only share things that have demonstrated to be of significance and trying to build a learning curve to understand exactly what needs to be shared and when.

In addition to these growing collaborative efforts, NCSD conducts outreach to countries with emerging cyber security and critical infrastructure protection programs and organizations. Through cooperation with the Department of State and other federal agencies, we participate in formal and informal bilateral discussions with countries and we participate in the cyber security components of organizations such as the Asia Pacific Economic Cooperation (APEC), the Organization of American States (OAS) and the Organization of Economic Cooperation and Development (OECD). DHS has also worked to establish cross border Critical Infrastructure Protection (CIP) arrangements that include cyber security in North America.

In general, NCSD is seeking to strengthen and build on existing bilateral, regional and multilateral information sharing efforts to facilitate the sharing of critical situational awareness information and begin to collaborate on priority strategic efforts to assess and mitigate cyber risk. There has been real progress in sharing information about the cyber security efforts being undertaken by nations and by global partnerships. However, work continues on enhancing and facilitating the regular and timely sharing of

Insider Notes: Threats, vulnerabilities and consequences are the components of risk assessment. While risk assessments should be conducted in all businesses, sectors and agencies, many existing risk methodologies have either been limited in scope or not widely implemented, because they often do not include cyber assets or cyber components of physical assets. A flexible, widely used risk methodology that addresses cyber security vulnerability is necessary to create the security practices applied to our physical and cyber infrastructure.

significant information necessary to help build cyber situational awareness among allied nations and global partners that benefits us here at home and in the international community.

PRIORITY TWO: APPLYING RISK MANAGEMENT TO CYBER SECURITY

The challenge before us is clear: how can companies, governments and individuals work together to address the multitude of cyber threats and vulnerabilities and demonstrate real progress in securing our cyber infrastructure? The answer to this question requires a dynamic risk-based approach that takes into account the unique consequences, vulnerabilities and threats of cyberspace. Analyzing risk to manage security priorities is one of Homeland Security's primary goals. As noted by Homeland Security Secretary Michael Chertoff, "Risk management must guide our decision-making as we examine how we can best organize to prevent, respond and recover from an attack."[1]

Threats, vulnerabilities and consequences are the components of risk assessment. While risk assessments should be conducted in all businesses, sectors and agencies, many existing risk methodologies have either been limited in scope or not widely implemented, because they often do not include cyber assets or cyber components of physical assets. A flexible, widely used risk methodology that addresses cyber security vulnerability is necessary to create the security practices applied to our physical and cyber infrastructure.

Given today's highly interconnected environment, a common approach is required to unify the protective activities within public, private and international entities and secure cyber infrastructure. Such an approach will allow risk comparison across assets and for more efficient resources allocation, as well as efficiently protecting cyber infrastructure. Recognizing this need, Homeland Security is leading the effort to protect the Nation's critical infrastructure through the risk management framework embodied in the National Infrastructure Protection Plan (NIPP); outreach and awareness; standards and best practices; training and education; research and development; and exercises.

THE NATIONAL INFRASTRUCTURE PROTECTION PLAN

The NIPP details how the public and private sectors will work together to identify, prioritize and conduct risk assessments of the 17 critical infrastructure and key resource (CI/KR) sectors. Homeland Security's risk-based approach is described in detail in the NIPP Base Plan that provides the unifying structure for the integration of CI/KR protection efforts into a single national program. It sets forth a Risk Management Framework for public and private sector partners to work together to produce a comprehensive, systematic and rational assessment of national or sector risk, which drives CI/KR risk mitigation and management activities. The NIPP includes a cross-sector cyber element that is a component of each sector and recognizes the IT Sector specifically as one of the 17 CI/KR sectors.

The cornerstone of the NIPP is the Risk Management Framework, which establishes the process for combining threat, vulnerability and consequence information to assess risk.

FIGURE 3: THE NIPP RISK MANAGEMENT FRAMEWORK

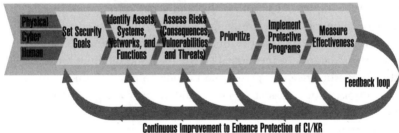

Continuous Improvement to Enhance Protection of CI/KR

The NIPP framework is composed of six specific activities:
- **Set security goals:** Define specific outcomes, conditions, end points or performance targets that collectively represent an effective security posture.
- **Identify assets, systems, networks and functions:** Develop an inventory of the individual assets, systems, networks and functions that make up the Nation's CI/KR, some of which may be located outside the U.S., and collect information on them, including dependencies, interdependencies and reliance on cyber systems.
- **Assess risks:** Determine which assets, systems, networks and func-

tions are critical by calculating risk, combining potential direct and indirect consequences of an attack (including dependencies and interdependencies associated with each identified asset), known vulnerabilities to various potential attack vectors and general or specific threat information.

- **Prioritize:** Aggregate and order assessment results to present a comprehensive picture of national CI/KR risk in order to establish protection priorities, provide the basis for planning and the informed allocation of resources.
- **Implement protective programs:** Select appropriate protective measures or programs and allocate funding and resources designed to address targeted priorities.
- **Measure effectiveness:** Incorporate metrics and other evaluation procedures at the national and sector levels to measure progress and assess effectiveness of the national CI/KR protection program.

The highly distributed and interconnected nature of cyber infrastructure, both physically and logically, requires that cyber protective actions and programs be implemented both within and across sectors. Homeland Security is committed to identifying and supporting a variety of protective initiatives and fostering international cooperation to secure the nation's cyber infrastructure. As mentioned above, the responsibilities for securing cyber infrastructure are dispersed and include both the producers and users of the infrastructure. Leaders at Homeland Security recognize that duality in implementing the NIPP framework and our efforts address both the IT Sector-specific responsibility and the cross-sector cyber element that applies to all sectors under the NIPP.

Information Technology Sector
The IT Sector, also referred to as the "IT Industrial Base," is comprised of the producers of hardware, software and IT services. Homeland Security is working collaboratively with our private and public sector partners in the IT Sector through the IT Sector Coordinating Council and Government Coordinating Council to determine their approach and criteria for each step of the framework. As with all infrastructure sectors, private stakeholder participation in the process is essential to developing and implementing an efficient and effective IT Sector Specific Plan (SSP). Furthermore, the

Internet has been identified as a key resource comprised of assets within both the IT and Telecommunications Sectors and is used by all sectors in varying degrees. The availability of the service is the responsibility of both the IT and Telecommunications Sectors, as all sectors rely upon and utilize the Internet.

Cross-Sector Cyber Element
While the producers of cyber infrastructure are addressed in the IT Sector, the cross-sector cyber element of the NIPP focuses on "consumers" of cyber infrastructure, including CI/KR sectors and their associated security partners. Each sector is responsible for securing its cyber infrastructure. The draft NIPP Base Plan addresses cyber security and the cross-sector cyber element of CI/KR protection across all 17 sectors. The NIPP also addresses specific cyber responsibilities for sector security partners, processes and initiatives to reduce cyber risk, and provides milestones and metrics to measure progress on enhancing the Nation's protection of our cyber infrastructure. The 17 CI/KR SSPs will further detail risk reduction strategies related to their respective critical cyber infrastructure.

All public and private sector organizations should develop and implement a cyber risk management strategy to reduce the risk to our cyber infrastructure. This strategy should include the following three components:

- **Identify cyber assets, systems, networks and functions** — A process should be defined and implemented to identify cyber assets and cyber elements of physical assets of potential sector, regional or national importance. Cyber assets represent a variety of hardware and software components, including business and control systems, networking equipment, database servers and software, and security

> **Insider Notes:** An organization's cyber risk mitigation strategy should be realistic and actionable with stakeholders fully engaged in the implementation. The NIPP framework is flexible enough to allow individual organizations to tailor it to meet their requirements. By securing portions of our cyber infrastructure across multiple organizations and the sectors, the overall infrastructure will become more resilient.

systems. The process for identifying cyber assets should be scalable, distributable and repeatable to ensure that it is practical, efficient and provides accurate results.

■ **Assess cyber risk** — Consequences, vulnerabilities and threats should be identified and analyzed to assess risk. Potential consequences should include those that result from reliance on cyber assets. Vulnerability assessments can be conducted on cyber assets using a variety of approaches, methodologies or criteria. Threat analysis should address those scenarios that are of highest concern.

■ **Implement protective programs to reduce risk** — Organizations should make decisions to implement protective programs based on their risk assessments and their desired security posture. While some risk may be acceptable, appropriate and effective protective measures will be necessary to balance risk and associated costs.

An organization's cyber risk mitigation strategy should be realistic and actionable with stakeholders fully engaged in the implementation. The NIPP framework is flexible enough to allow individual organizations to tailor it to meet their requirements. By securing portions of our cyber infrastructure across multiple organizations and the sectors, the overall infrastructure will become more resilient.

No one can protect the entire cyber infrastructure alone. Homeland Security will continue to partner with state, local, tribal and international governments, businesses, industries and sectors to mitigate the risk associated with cyber consequences, vulnerabilities and threats. Homeland Security applauds the efforts of businesses and government agencies thus far, and encourages them to continue partnering with their Sector Specific Agencies and respective coordinating councils. Together, all infrastructure stakeholders can reduce risk and improve the overall security of our cyber infrastructure.

OUTREACH AND AWARENESS

Governments and companies in the private sector are not the only areas of concern with regard to managing the cyber risk. Every computer connected to the Internet is a potential risk. Mitigating cyber risk is the responsibility of everyone who uses a computer or wireless device, from consumers to small businesses. We reduce our Nation's overall cyber risk when each user understands the changing threats, how to prepare for these threats and how to report incidents to the proper authorities.

Homeland Security is focused on raising cyber security awareness levels and disseminating timely and actionable information to the public, private sector and international stakeholders. By leveraging traditional methods of outreach, such as the mainstream media and strategic partnerships, the Federal Trade Commission (www.OnGuardOnline.gov) and the National Cyber Security Alliance (NCSA) (www.StaySafeOnline.org), NCSD is proactively educating individual computer users as neutral and trusted sources on how they can protect themselves, and empowering them to report cyber attacks that they experience.

STANDARDS AND BEST PRACTICES

To allow clear information sharing, security experts need a common language and terminology to discuss and agree upon technical details. A simple example is a worm that was set to attack systems in early 2006. This worm had multiple common names, leading to some confusion throughout the technical communities. US-CERT stepped in and assigned this worm the Common Malware Enumeration (CME) identifier of CME-24.

NCSD sponsors and develops cyber security guidance and best practices documents in partnership with public and private entities and participates in various interagency committees and working groups, as well as standards bodies. Key partnerships in this area include the National Institute of Standards and Technology (NIST) Computer Security Division (CSD) and the Center for Internet Security (CIS).

Insider Notes: The combination of raw cyber information and interpretive analysis are the keys to improving our response to a cyber incident. In this regard, there has been a constant push and pull between the needs of the analysts and the proprietary needs of private companies. Today, information sharing is based on informal thresholds, public information and relationships with specific partners.

The InterNational Committee for Information Technology Standards (INCITS) is the primary U.S. focus of standardization in the field of information and communications technologies encompassing storage, processing, transfer, display, management, organization and retrieval of information. NCSD actively participates in this effort through its involvement in the Technical Advisory Group for Cyber Security Standards and Development.

TRAINING AND EDUCATION

Making an investment in the future of security is a key part of reducing vulnerabilities over time. In order to protect the critical infrastructure, our nation must focus resources on training a talented and innovative pool of citizens that can specialize in securing our cyber infrastructure. To this end, NCSD and the National Security Agency (NSA) have collaborated to amplify an existing, successful program. The Centers of Academic Excellence in Information Assurance Education Program (CAEIAE) have partnered with NCSD and the NSA to promote higher education in information assurance in order to increase the number of information assurance professionals. There are currently 67 universities in 27 states and the District of Columbia designated as CAEIAEs.

NCSD and the National Science Foundation (NSF) co-sponsor the Scholarship for Service Program (Cyber Corps) providing two-year scholarships in information assurance, and support the expansion of information assurance course offerings at higher education institutions. Currently, more than 300 students from 25 colleges are enrolled in Cyber Corps.

Additionally, NCSD is launching development of the Information Systems Security (ISS) Professionals Common Body of Knowledge to promote uniform training standards that can be used for IT security certification programs in the public and private sectors.

EXERCISES

NCSD is committed to protecting our nation's infrastructure and working together with all levels of government and the private sector to coordinate cyber security efforts and to protect our Nation's information infrastructure. One of the mechanisms used to understand how to enhance our nation's cyber preparedness and better manage risk is the exercise program.

The recent Cyber Storm exercise conducted in February 2006 is a clear example of how Homeland Security examined response, coordination and recovery mechanisms to a simulated cyber-event within international, federal, state and local governments, in conjunction with the private sector. The exercise simulated a sophisticated cyber attack through a series of scenarios directed against critical infrastructures such as energy and transportation and the federal, state and international governments, with the intent of disrupting government operations and degrading public confidence.

By performing an exercise such as Cyber Storm, Homeland Security can examine the national cyber incident response and critical information sharing paths and mechanisms among public and private sectors, as well as identify policy issues that affect response and recovery. Exercises can also provide insight into ways to improve and promote public and private sector interaction toward enhancing situational awareness that supports public and private sector decision making, communicating appropriate information to key stakeholders and the public, and planning and implementing appropriate response and recovery activities.

Coordination among federal and state government agencies and the private sector is the underpinning of incident response, to ensure the leveraging, sharing and collaborating needed to enhance coordinated preparedness. All aspects of building an effective cyber defense require this coordination, including situational awareness, attribution, analysis, response and recovery. Lessons learned from Cyber Storm will help improve these efforts.

LOOKING TO THE FUTURE: IMPROVING SITUATIONAL AWARENESS

How can we improve our understanding of the health of the Internet? The combination of raw cyber information and interpretive analysis are the keys to improving our response to a cyber incident. In this regard, there has been a constant push and pull between the needs of the analysts and the proprietary needs of private companies. Today, information sharing is based on informal thresholds, public information and relationships with specific partners.

To improve the kind of raw cyber information and analysis that needs to be shared and when, Homeland Security is searching for methods to improve our situational awareness with its partners: federal government agency first responders, the federal government-based incident response team community and the sector specific ISACs. Recently, some of the representatives of the ISPs in the private sector who are partners with the Internet Disruption Working Group (IDWG) have joined this dialogue. The members of this partnership bring a variety of viewpoints and see a wide variety of raw data.

At one level, there is discussion in this partnership about what information and resources the government needs, particularly because the federal government determines the threshold for triggering national cyber response coordination when there is a cyber Incident of National Significance. On the other hand, it is clear among the private sector partners, such as the ISPs, that they handle numerous cyber incidents every day. They see a tremendous amount of raw data, malicious activity and other problems, and are accustomed to managing incidents largely on their own, or on relatively rare occasions, by working with law enforcement or US-CERT.

Therefore, while ISPs want to know what information the government requires at certain pre-determined levels of seriousness, it is critically important for the government to know from them what they deem unusual. This includes problems that are threatening multiple networks and those that appear to pose a potential threat to government systems and the systems of critical infrastructure owners and operators.

The challenge to improving situational awareness is the need to facilitate the sharing of raw information and analysis. Our Nation cannot wait for a person, an independent company, an ISP or a State government to report significant malicious activity until they think it actually constitutes a cyber Incident of National (or international) Significance. This necessitates enhancing trust relationships and building others, both within government and between government and the private sector. Programs such as the NIPP Framework provide a protected arena to grow trust and relationships. As the NIPP becomes more established and matures, so will these trusted relationships. From these trusted relationships, more information will be exchanged and national situational awareness will improve.

Improved situational awareness will help prevent incidents from escalating to a national issue. Many individual ISPs can identify activity that, while it may not yet be obviously national in scope, does pose a significant risk to critical systems. It is those seemingly less serious situations, that appear not yet to be of national importance, which may need some response depending on the availability of information from additional sources. If these private sector entities are active with their sector ISACs, those situations, identified from different entities, can be combined by centralized entities such as US-CERT or the ISAC Council, which collect information from all the ISACs. As the data is increased to these key groups, it needs to be synthesized in a valuable way that can facilitate the ability to respond and mitigate this kind of malicious activity before it becomes of national significance.

While this article has posited that information sharing is currently based on loose thresholds, public information and relationships with specific partners, it appears that things are evolving toward more systemized and predictable information flows. Trusted partners are developing ways to communicate regularly and productively about what they are seeing in cyberspace.

This model for the sharing of this type of analysis data should be encouraged and enhanced, at least within trusted public/private partnerships, with an emphasis on establishing and growing regional relationships. With such information in hand, if the receiving entity sees malicious activity, they can reach back to the source of the information and look for the particular data that corresponds to it to identify a connection or a signature in common, or a common source IP address, and so forth. It may then be identified as the type of activity that an existing tool or a newly fashioned tool can identify and mitigate.

The long-term benefit to this model is that when combined, shared reports can provide a more accurate cyber risk or threat picture. Relevant information can be shared with the most relevant parties on a wider basis than before. For example, if appropriate, an increased amount of information can be shared with the antivirus community, which can then act more quickly in order to protect thousands from the particular variant. In addition, this information may help law enforcement, the Intelligence community or the computer security incident response community to identify the target of the malicious activity, as well as the origin of its source and the vulnerabilities that are being exploited.

Each company can do their part to increase situational awareness. Homeland Security applauds our current private sector partners and encourages those in industry that are not involved to take part in the process of increasing our situational awareness. The NIPP Framework, Sector Specific Councils within the NIPP and the sector specific ISACs are established forums for dialogue and action within the sectors, and to governments at all levels.

The federal government is working to increase the "value loop" for information sharing. In order to receive more granular information, we are developing improved articulation of our information requirements. This will enable government to share additional valuable information across the government and out to our trusted partners in the private sector.

Improved information sharing and data analysis will help us arrive at our mutual goal of understanding our true situation on the Internet. Our partnership will continue to take a broader look; not only of what they have and what they are sharing, but also learning what other information is needed to paint a more robust picture of Internet health.

STRATEGIC PRIORITIES

NCSD has created two strategic priorities to protect our nation against cyber attack, but no one organization can protect the entire cyber infrastructure alone. Homeland Security will continue to enhance existing partnerships and build new ones with federal, state, local and international governments, businesses and industries to mitigate the risk associated with cyber consequences, vulnerabilities and threats.

Homeland Security applauds the efforts of businesses and government agencies thus far, and encourages them to continue partnering and bringing their ideas and energy to Sector Specific Agencies and respective coordinating councils. By working together, all infrastructure stakeholders can reduce risk and improve the overall security of our cyber infrastructure.

The federal government has come a long way since the development of the *National Strategy to Secure Cyberspace* and the launch of the Department of Homeland Security in 2003. Nonetheless, we can't rest in this ever-changing arena. Homeland Security has frameworks in place for cyber security response and risk management, and is working now to implement the tenets of those frameworks in current programs and partnerships. US-CERT Operations, the NCRCG, the NIPP and related risk mitigation programs are key elements in our efforts to take our nation's cyber preparedness capabilities to the next level.

■ ■ ■

Donald A. "Andy" Purdy is Acting Director of Cyber Security for the U.S. Department of Homeland Security. Cyber incidents and information can be reported to NCSD's US-CERT at soc@us-cert.gov. For additional information about US-CERT, visit www.us-cert.gov.

[1] Remarks by Secretary Michael Chertoff at the George Washington University Homeland Security Policy Institute on March 16, 2005.

[2]

RAISING INFORMATION EXCHANGE TO A SMARTER LEVEL

To ensure proactive cyber security, decision makers increasingly require actionable information delivered in real time. Meeting this goal requires a paradigm shift in how information is gathered, stored and analyzed. When applied to certain data processes, technology can provide the "intelligent information exchange" that today's government manager demands.

"YOU CAN NEVER SOLVE A PROBLEM ON THE LEVEL ON WHICH IT WAS CREATED."
— Albert Einstein

by GREGORY N. AKERS

Today's cyber outlaws adopt constantly changing tactics. To stay a step ahead of security threats, government IT managers must adopt a new way of thinking. What's required is the ability to analyze data as it's being collected, and simultaneously put this data into historical context. The goal is to decide in real time what's actionable and what's not. That's where the

DATA SNAPSHOT

Does your agency/organization depend on open source information (e.g., logos, newspapers, TV reports, blogs) to augment what is collected from traditional sources in support of the agency's/organization's mission?

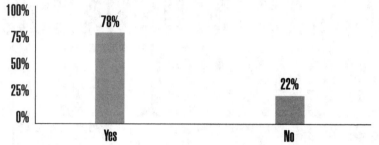

The vast majority of government agencies rely on open source information.

Download the complete research study for free at www.theblackbooks.com
Source: 2005 Larstan Business Reports

emerging capability of "intelligent information exchange" plays an enormous role.

Typically in the past, information has been utilized by a well-defined collection, analytical and decision process. This process has been followed, regardless of the eventual purpose or benefit to the recipient, or whether that recipient is a first responder, defense department or a civilian agency. Consequently, the freshness of this information is generally known and can be controlled to some degree.

However, the situation is different for much of the open source information that can be compiled from newspapers, blogs and the like. Within these sources, the information has, in and of itself, a temporal basis. But frankly, this data may feature components that are trustworthy and others that are not. These degrees of veracity may change over time, as other information is either collected or becomes available later.

Decision makers often are put into a position of using available information to make rational decisions about how to act. The information available can come from both predictable processes as well as more volatile and unpredictable ones. Their utility must be determined by the user and applied to the decision process appropriately. Technology alone can't take the place of higher reasoning in that assessment, but it can assist a human in making decisions in a more precise and timely manner. Technology can apply analytical insight, for greater perspective and deeper understanding.

Part of the problem that analysts of all types encounter is the need to distill waves of information in a timely and expeditious fashion into something that is consumable and usable by a human. Sometimes this may mean that technology needs to speed up the processing, other times it may mean that technology needs to slow the process down and clarify its direction.

Situations often arise when analysts find that they can reapply information they have used before and greatly reduce the overall collection process. What I am suggesting is that technology can apply rules and "learn" from previous situational processing. This knowledge can be incorporated to produce an outcome that a human would otherwise not be able to extract at all or, at least, not in a timely enough fashion to take the appropriate action.

For example, in the case of Hurricane Katrina, there was probably plenty of raw information available days in advance — e.g., weather circumstances, the structural analysis of levees and the current state of water flow patterns. This data would have been sufficient enough for an analyst, with the opportunity to work through it, to build a case for taking different and

Insider Notes: Situations often arise when analysts find that they can reapply information they have used before and greatly reduce the overall collection process. What I am suggesting is that technology can apply rules and "learn" from previous situational processing. This knowledge can be incorporated to produce an outcome that a human would otherwise not be able to extract at all or, at least, not in a timely enough fashion to take the appropriate action.

THE NEED TO SHORTEN THE LOOP BETWEEN INFORMATION CAPTURE, ITS ANALYSIS AND THE APPLICATION OF DECISIVE ACTION IS AN OVERARCHING CONSIDERATION FOR ALL ANALYSTS.

decisive action in terms of evacuation, protection, public alerts and all of the measures that, in retrospect, should have been pursued. However, the problem was in making the data useful and then making a decision to use it in a way that would have had an timely impact.

In most situations, there is a period of time in which the major players can go back and use hindsight effectively to capture lessons learned, and apply them to a decision rule set. However, people forget, or fail to think about, the importance of the information, and it gets lost forever. Below are ways to avoid this pitfall.

THE IMPORTANCE OF ATTRIBUTION

Attributable details can limit the usefulness and timeliness of information. For example, a key issue with Katrina was in weather reporting. Weather reporting is an imprecise science. It tends to feed on itself and is too often couched in terminology that sells newspapers or drives TV ratings. There are many aspects of weather reporting that are impacted by the source of the information. Unfortunately, agencies, first responders and others become the unwary benefactors of this information whether they want to or not. Canonical details have ways of affecting the use of the information and it is often not clear that it is even being done. Of course, as events come and go, the information's relevance is lost, as happened with Katrina.

In the case of intelligence, defense and civilian agencies, "attributable" details are particularly important. "Attribution" means "Who said it, why they said it, and why they meant to say it." The later part, the "Why they meant to say it," can often become lost. There are circumstances where someone may provide misinformation deliberately. This relates to propaganda. Misinformation is useful because it causes a certain effect. For example, the manner in which today's news sources discuss the Middle

East and Iraq often relates to opinions of what is happening there. It is apparent that information is manipulated and the attributed source needs to be a strong consideration.

SHORTENING THE LOOP

The need to shorten the loop between information capture, its analysis and the application of decisive action is an overarching consideration for all analysts. In the manufacturing world, there exists an ODOO loop. ODOO stands for Observe, Decide, Operationalize and Optimize. Many manufacturing facilities go through these very finite procedural steps to get to a desired outcome. This process is cyclic. Once the optimizing step is completed, the observation step starts over again. It is almost like the scientific process of hypothesizing, experimenting and so forth.

In many cases, technology can shorten long loops, turning them into hours, minutes, seconds or even sub-seconds. Technology operates at those sub-second rates, so the goal is to get those loops as short as possible, while maintaining required checks and balances along the way and including human intervention at the end to facilitate decisive action.

An important consideration is how technology can derive data that is relevant to a situation. There are a number of ways it can accomplish this. First, information can be time stamped at its inception, when it gets used and, certainly, when it becomes obsolete. Assessing the time benefit of information is critical. Also critical is determining how frequently information is used. If frequency of use drops off, that information is probably not as useful as it was before. However, the timeframes between when this information was acted upon becomes very important. From this, the benefit and timeliness of that information, based upon who is using it, when

Insider Notes: In many cases, technology can shorten long loops, turning them into hours, minutes, seconds or even sub-seconds. Technology operates at those sub-second rates, so the goal is to get those loops as short as possible, while maintaining required checks and balances along the way and including human intervention at the end to facilitate decisive action.

DATA SNAPSHOT

Does your agency/organization primarily depend on other agencies/organizations for information to support its mission?

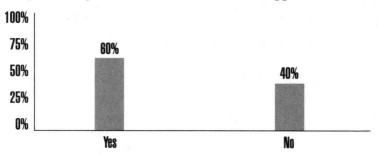

The majority of government agencies also rely on other agencies for information.

Download the complete research study for free at www.theblackbooks.com
Source: 2005 Larstan Business Reports

they are using it and what subsequent action is taken, can be observed and it can be put into this decision process model.

THE ROLE OF OPEN SOURCE INFORMATION

The days of controlling the collection of information for decision making with the expectation that all the information needed will be in predefined locations are long over. Today, more information sources arrive in a passive fashion and will not have to be actively gathered. For example, information comes in from the weather service, but critical information also may arrive from a number of other places. In the Katrina experience, reported flooding situations were already occurring in certain places days before the storm. This should have been looked at, creating a sense of concern that this storm would, at the very least, compound an existing problem and pose a potential catastrophe.

In other situations an analyst may end up with information culled from people chatting on the web or people blogging information. Traditionally, a person in search of data would need to look for it directly. Now, they only need to search for data that is highly critical, highly leveraged or specific to the topic, and then go to this open source channel for the other information that they need. In this scenario, the problem is that the reduction process and analytic process become more difficult because there are more dimensions to the information to be processed.

For example, in the wake of Katrina, several entities discussed placing sensor infrastructures into the dams, bridges and levees. That became the problem. With this amount of overlap, they could "over sensor" the same piece of infrastructure. They needed to think about leveraging existing information in a targeted way, to produce exactly the analysis they needed for an appropriate action.

TECHNOLOGY AS AN ENABLER

The analysis process for security information needs to start at the time it is collected. In my company, Cisco, we regularly get firewall hits where hackers "turn the knob on the door" to determine vulnerability to a particular virus or other malicious activity. What we have typically done is warehouse that information and then post-process it.

The problem is that the information complexity compounds under the load and becomes difficult to use. The message here is that there is a real need for technology to start processing that information at the time that it is collected. This process may acquire additional benefits or may be grayed over time, but it needs to be appropriately processed at the outset. Therefore, there is a need to install technology that can do the analytical work, for categorizing and time stamping, as soon as possible once the information is gathered.

> **Insider Notes:** The point is quickly reached where attempts are made to provide programming or information in a format and manner that can respond to a particular question in real time. This is the kind of process that needs to be discouraged, since there is also the point where information will be needed in ways that can't be predicted. This creates the need for a process that positions and characterizes information appropriately and allows it to be tapped.

THE ENTRENCHED MODEL FOR INFORMATION ANALYSIS IS NO LONGER APPROPRIATE FOR TODAY'S INCREASINGLY CLEVER CYBER THREAT.

In this process, technology needs to be viewed as an enabler and an expeditor in helping decision-making. Typically, attempts are made to try to replace the elements of the processes that are traditionally used by humans to make decisions with technology. There is a need to look at those processes cyclically, as with an ODOO loop, to refine and improve the process. Once optimization is complete, there is the need to re-observe and go through the process again, recursively. This will actually allow the human the ability to refine and change that process and optimize it over time. There also will be times where it's inappropriate to simply replace the process that was there before, regardless of whether it was done by human or machine.

MARRYING APPLICATIONS TO NETWORK INFRASTRUCTURE

Today, the application and the network are considered as two separate components that run somewhat independent of each another. The user is then faced with an integration process where one application, whether legacy or designed specifically for a new purpose, has to be bilaterally integrated with other applications. The network can communicate information but does not participate in the special work of integration.

This bifurcation is a classic problem, whether it is an accounts payable system integrating with the payroll system, or a decision-making system with subsequent action triggers that determine that a storm is coming, the gates should be closed and a decision to evacuate made. These applications are typically built independent of one another and they have to be put together. Marrying the application and the network recognizes the fact that messaging between these applications must be done — and this messaging can be standardized.

Therefore, the network can take advantage of the messaging that the application needs to do in the standard format and expedite the routing of it, both in terms of speed as well as in terms of work loading. This means that if a particular analytical tool can't handle the information needed for analysis now, the network can redirect the request to other available resources. For example, if a particular computing resource can't handle the processing of a satellite detail of the levee system in New Orleans and look for potential problem areas, the network can move this request over to a system that can, and still get back to the same point to make a decision in a timely fashion.

This need for application and network infrastructure to collaborate to address a more secure and more trusted computing environment for information sharing is most notable within the Department of Defense (DOD). The DOD is particularly challenged in that it must protect sensitive information from certain individuals and organizations while simultaneously sharing it within a coalition environment. Within this community there are directives that establish compartmentalization of information within the same level of classification. This information-sharing environment requires a policy-based architecture that can enforce rules, policies and privileges by controlling access and protecting data across the entire network.

This challenge was met by the development of a Coalition Architecture that combined Commercial Off The Shelf (COTS) products from Cisco, Microsoft, EMC and other companies. This architecture took the coalition environment to the next step by compartmentalizing information based on coalitions at the same level of classification. This architecture leveraged the

Insider Notes: The problem is that the information complexity compounds under the load and becomes difficult to use. The message here is that there is a real need for technology to start processing that information at the time that it is collected. This process may acquire additional benefits or may be grayed over time, but it needs to be appropriately processed at the outset. Therefore, there is a need to install technology that can do the analytical work, for categorizing and time stamping, as soon as possible once the information is gathered.

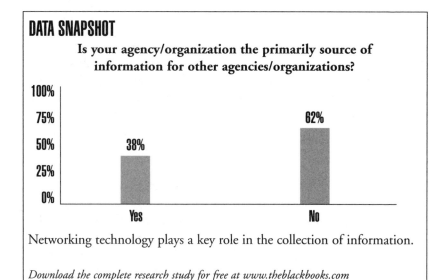

DATA SNAPSHOT

Is your agency/organization the primarily source of information for other agencies/organizations?

Networking technology plays a key role in the collection of information.

Download the complete research study for free at www.theblackbooks.com
Source: 2005 Larstan Business Reports

network infrastructure with the application to provide a more secure development and exchange of information within a dynamic environment. It allows members of established and ad hoc coalitions to share information freely, while protecting stored and in-transit data by enforcing security policies and procedures. Alliance members become part of a dynamic information-sharing environment that has the capabilities of withholding proprietary information from administrators without a "need to know."

REAL TIME, ALL THE TIME

Responding to time based information in real time is analogous to addressing numerous changing "what if" scenarios. Unfortunately, the approach currently taken is that if a question could be asked, then the information needs to be pre-positioned in a way that will allow that question to be responded to. This gets into the business of trying to predict action, whether it takes the form of a database query system or scanning channels on a satellite TV.

The point is quickly reached where attempts are made to provide programming or information in a format and manner that can respond to a particular question in real time. This is the kind of process that needs to be discouraged, since there is also the point where information will be needed in ways that can't be predicted. This creates the need for a process that positions and characterizes information appropriately and allows it to be tapped.

This is not fundamentally different from on-demand entertainment services currently offered by some cable and satellite systems. These services do not necessarily try to predict exactly what the viewer wants to see. Instead, they try to make things available and then provide viewer access upon demand. This is how technology can be a benefit in security. It can allow information to be extracted via a data tape, a portal, etc., without having to know the predefined question or having characterized it in any particular way.

INSURING AGAINST VULNERABILITIES

Once information is extracted and the decision-making begun, a decision history or record is built up over time. This creates the situation where one might begin to create questions like "Well, what if someone comes behind me and sees what I am doing?" For example, within the financial community, an analyst from one company conducting research on a particular market segment might not want competitors knowing about this research. The question becomes how to obfuscate the fact that this research is being done.

If the analyst visits a web site, his interests can be tracked, unless he is protected against spyware. (The purpose of spyware is to determine users' interests, so something else can be offered that might be of use to them, but the perpetrators also gain some insight into these uses.) Either for privacy reasons or at the very least for competitive reasons, no one wants oth-

> **Insider Notes:** At each step along the way of an information exchange, a risk quotient should be applied. This quotient can be mathematically based or not. Regardless, it must determine potential losses incurred from any security breach (in terms of dollars, lives, etc.), and what it will cost to protect the information. By assessing these risk and protection quotients, equilibrium can be reached.

ers to know what they are looking at. That information may be very useful to a competitor. And no one wants that type of visibility shared.

A ROAD MAP TO THE PARADIGM SHIFT

Below is a three-step process for forging "intelligent information exchange" systems that facilitate better and faster decision-making:

❶ Develop a Risk Model for Measuring Information Utility

This is fairly straightforward notion; it is the implementation that is difficult. The availability of information, whether it is open source or at the highest levels of government security, is put at risk when it is exchanged between one party and another. The only information that is not at risk is that which is not exchanged. At some point, when a person or an entity makes a decision to share and exchange information, they also make a conscience or unconscious decision that that information, which they had previously protected, will now be shared or exchanged with someone who may put it at risk in ways not intended.

At each step along the way of an information exchange, a risk quotient should be applied. This quotient can be mathematically based or not. Regardless, it must determine potential losses incurred from any security breach (in terms of dollars, lives, etc.), and what it will cost to protect the information. By assessing these risk and protection quotients, equilibrium can be reached. When an exchange passes beyond the point of an acceptable risk, an acceptable level of disclosure or cost to protect must be a conscious decision. Technology can be used to derive equilibrium among the various aspects of risk, disclosure and cost to protect.

❷ Move the Analytical Process up the Information Chain

It's crucial to push the analytical process as far up toward the gathering process as possible. The dissemination aspect of information leading from analytics must be technology enabled for speedy, experiential decision-making. Acquiring and using analytical computer resources that project as far as possible into the future must be considered. Available computing and analytical capabilities need to be viewed on a continuum, as opposed to just for specific tasks.

In this regard, the value of public and private partnership can't be overstated. Open source information speaks directly to this need. Public-private partnerships exist in terms of information exchange, but there also exists the opportunity to extend this model into the realm of security. The government is the user, and private industry is the technology provider. Companies are the enablers that build systems, create technology and help users do their jobs.

❸ Leverage Advanced Research and Development

Innovation must be valued, nurtured and applied. Whether it derives from academia, the government or corporations, advanced research and development must be driven by the needs of the user. It's up to the government user to identify the truly difficult problems. It can be a current problem or one that is over the horizon and not addressed by technology. Industry then needs to inform government about the relevant shortfalls in private sector technology, and how to remedy them.

Problems must be viewed as an overarching research agenda. At the end of the day, no one will get better at doing their job or helping to create the next type of security measure, unless all available resources are being utilized, in concert.

These three steps aren't the complete answer; they're only a start. They require continual review and refinement. The risk model must be regularly assessed according to current conditions and appropriately enhanced. New and better ways must be found to push the analytical process even further upstream. Although these steps are proscriptive, they also define a process that must be incessantly calibrated according to evolving security challenges.

The entrenched model for information analysis is no longer appropriate for today's increasingly clever cyber threat. This model must be reconfigured, to quickly provide decision makers with the information they need. Instead of "gather, store and analyze," we need to "gather, analyze and store."

■ ■ ■

Greg Akers runs Cisco's Global Government Solutions group, to deliver platforms, capabilities and value added support to Cisco's government customers. Akers also leads several strategic Cisco Security Programs. Within Cisco, he has formed the Critical Infrastructure Assurance Group, or CIAG. The primary goal of CIAG is to further advance Critical Infrastructure Protection through research, education and training for the sole purpose of improving global infrastructure security. In addition, Mr. Akers has responsibility for Cisco's Corporate Security Programs, which ensure the integrity, confidentiality and availability of critical information and computing assets.

Akers also plays a crucial role as an Internet security and critical infrastructure protection interface with the U.S. Federal Government and Cisco customers. As an example of his leadership in the government interface/Internet security area, he served as president of the IT-Information Sharing and Analysis Center (ISAC) in 2002. Akers also is a member of the National White-Collar Crime Board and the Board of Directors of the East Carolina Infraguard. He can be reached at gakers@cisco.com.

[3]
SECURITY THROUGH CONSISTENCY

Technological consistency, even more than rigid standards, is a crucial component to enhancing cyber security. Here's how the computer industry can leverage the power of the federal government to foster IT consistency – and in the process, improve software security.

> **"MY GOAL IN SAILING ISN'T TO BE BRILLIANT OR FLASHY IN INDIVIDUAL RACES, JUST TO BE CONSISTENT OVER THE LONG RUN."**
> — Dennis Conner, sailing champion and four-time winner of the America's Cup

by MARY ANN DAVIDSON

Government at all levels is the quintessential buyer of information technology, with more collective buying power than any other sector. However, the government neglects to leverage its economic clout to insist on high-quality, robust products. Agencies often complain about how bad products are when, to ameliorate this problem, they should merely stop buying inferior products.

MOST OF WHAT THE GOVERNMENT DOES TODAY HAS AN I.T. BACKBONE, INCLUDING ITS WAR FIGHTING SYSTEMS. THIS MEANS THAT, ESSENTIALLY, THE NETWORK HAS BECOME THE BATTLEFIELD.

Government can use its vast procurement power to entice the software industry to build better products in a consistent way.

In extraordinary cases, this can and has been done with standards. But more often, government can create positive change by:
- insisting upon vendors' use of a secure practice of software development
- only purchasing software that meets quality levels for security
- only purchasing software with independent vetting of security claims
- only purchasing software that can be delivered in a locked-down configuration

It would be impossible to actually standardize software development practices. There are near-religious arguments over whether method A is better than method B, and no way to determine that one method works better than the other. What government can do is to use purchasing vehicles to find out what vendors are doing, and look for vendors doing the right thing. Government has far more power than it thinks to change IT market dynamics by requiring better development practice as a condition of purchase.

GOVERNMENT AT RISK

However you measure it, the government has an increased risk to its IT systems, a risk that is typically reflected in the flunking grade so many agencies receive on their yearly security report cards. There are many reasons for that. One reason is that the government is using Commercial Off-The-Shelf software (COTS) to a greater degree than ever before: in fact, its critical systems depend on commercial software.

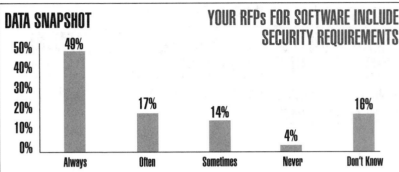

DATA SNAPSHOT

YOUR RFPs FOR SOFTWARE INCLUDE SECURITY REQUIREMENTS

Only half of those asked said their RFPs include security requirements; given the nature of the data the government collects and protects, this should be much higher. Amending the Federal Acquisition Regulations so that security is a purchasing criterion is a good start.
Download the complete research study for free at www.theblackbooks.com
Source: 2005 Larstan Business Reports

Consequently, the assurance (the proven security-worthiness) of commercial software is now of critical importance. Moreover, the provenance is often unknown. That is, the federal government relies on integrators who buy/build/incorporate third party software that was built God-knows-how, in God-knows-where, by God-knows-whom. To a large degree, the security of all of this important, mission-critical software is in the hands of commercial vendors who probably did not think they were participating in "national security" when they built and delivered the software.

The current state of the IT industry is that no vendor can accurately state that its products are engineered to be reliably secure. Nor can they state that their products are so easy to secure that it is almost impossible to operate them in an unsecured manner. The risks of the industry continuing in this manner are high, and getting higher.

> **Insider Notes:** The current state of the IT industry is that no vendor can accurately state that its products are engineered to be reliably secure. Nor can they state that their products are so easy to secure that it is almost impossible to operate them in an unsecured manner. The risks of the industry continuing in this manner are high, and getting higher.

THE ABSENCE OF BASELINE SECURITY AND "SECURABILITY" IS ONE OF THE FUNDAMENTAL PROBLEMS WITH COMMERCIAL SOFTWARE. IT IS GENERALLY DIFFICULT FOR CUSTOMERS TO FIND OUT HOW TO LOCK DOWN AN APPLICATION.

The cost of bad security is already astronomical. The National Institute of Standards and Technology (NIST) has estimated that the cost of bad security in the United States alone was as high as $59 billion per year. Even more dangerous is the fact that hacking trends have graduated from "hacking to show off" towards "hacking for more malicious purposes." This includes not only cyber crime, but also activity by hostile nation-states. Former Secretary of Homeland Security Tom Ridge succinctly stated that: "A few lines of code can wreak more havoc than a bomb."

ONE BIG GOVERNMENT NETWORK

The government has responded to its intelligence shortcomings in part by strongly encouraging the sharing of data and the elimination of agency IT stovepipes. IT security becomes even more critical when there are no physical barriers between networks. While the move from "need to know" to "need to share" is necessary for larger national security purposes, ironically, the destruction of these stovepipes of information may also raise the IT risk posture disproportionately. As the government puts more information into its networks, the greater its risk exposure will become, just as putting more traffic on a bridge raises the risk exposure of a bridge not designed to handle the load.

For example, the Department of Defense (DOD) is now considering linking together its physically separate networks as they move to a Global Information Grid (GIG). This is a major undertaking that can have a decisive tactical and strategic impact. It will also create a huge risk. Right now, it is impossible to physically get into some of the networks from the Internet because they are not physically connected to the Internet. Also, access is restricted to those already on that network. This cuts the riffraff out because people on these top-secret networks have security clearances, and data is classified both hierarchically and by compartments.

Note that these networks can be violated, but there is a big difference between the scale of violation possible on an unconnected network and one that is on the Internet. The physical barriers provide a natural defensive perimeter. Remove the natural defensive perimeter and there is much more territory to defend, just as taking the vault door off the bank vault means that more work is necessary to determine friend from foe, and more means of egress to watch and defend against. The DOD wants to get the goodies inside their bank vault out to the people who need it. But, by taking the doors off the vault to get the money out faster, they have much more to defend in order to ensure that they don't get robbed.

THE NETWORK BECOMES THE BATTLEFIELD

Most of what the government does today has an IT backbone, including its war fighting systems. This means that, essentially, the network has become the battlefield. The military now needs to be able to assess basic situational awareness, both on the battlefield and on its network. Military leaders must be able to determine the size and presence of the enemy on the other side of the hill as well as the potential presence and activity of the enemy on the network. This is a general problem that everyone with a network has, but its potential effects are magnified in the case of the DOD.

The DOD vision is to have its networks reside on the global information grid instead of remaining physically partitioned from each other. They would, ideally, like to have interesting intelligent intercepts and other pieces of relevant (redacted) information that may be highly sensitive made available all the way down to the war fighter within a wireless domain. This must be accomplished while maintaining the right security classifica-

Insider Notes: The computer industry must help by providing better quality software. This means delivering software with better security functionality that also adheres to existing standards. This will allow some of these applications to work together and provide better early warning and situational awareness. If not, the government is in trouble.

tions. In essence, the DOD plans to move from a policy of need-to-know, where all information is held close to the chest, to one of need-to-share, where information is being pushed out to the people who need it. This new policy creates severe time sensitivity, whereby decision makers can't afford a wait of days or weeks for information declassification.

Adding to this problem is the fact that the DOD is also busy creating ad hoc networks on the fly to support the coalitions through which much foreign policy is now conducted. The reasons for this are sound, but the coalition model carries a high risk of network violation. Physically separating networks buys a lot of security that is lost when they are exposed to the Internet. By opening these networks to the Internet and other nations, the battlefield can actually evolve to the network. Why should an enemy target soldiers when their ability to wage war can be enhanced by attacking your network? Once into the network, an enemy can change information, retarget missile batteries, and accomplish all kinds of mischief. The worst effect might well be corrupting some of the data war fighters rely upon, thereby causing those who rely on networked information to regard all information as suspect.

In accomplishing this new policy of sharing, the government is to a large extent going to be stuck, across the board, with what the commercial software industry can provide in terms of security. That's because most software is COTS or relies on a COTS underpinning (e.g., even custom applications will use standard commercial operating systems, and standard commercial components such as databases, application servers and directories). Now, the risk posture has gone way up. Not all of this risk can be mitigated, since commercial software was not, in general, designed for that aggressive an environment.

However, government can insist on better security out-of-the-box and more (and more provable) security-worthiness over time. The computer industry must help by providing better quality software. This means delivering software with better security functionality that also adheres to existing standards. This will allow some of these applications to work together and provide better early warning and situational awareness. If not, the government is in trouble.

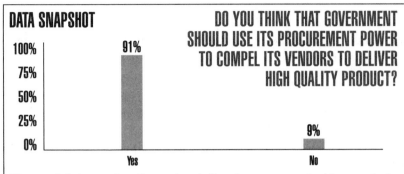

The overwhelming number of respondents believe the government should use purchasing power to compel better product from their vendors.

Download the complete research study for free at www.theblackbooks.com

Source: 2005 Larstan Business Reports

Regardless of how we got here, it is apparent that this "assurance problem" will not be comprehensively addressed without some forcing function.

Moreover, this is not solely a government problem. Almost everyone in corporate America has a similar issue. If any company is asked to identify at this particular second:

- Who is connected to their network?
- What is their security posture?
- What is vulnerable and what isn't?
- What is going on in the network?
- Whether they should be concerned?

They couldn't tell you. The issue is, why is it so hard to do? The capability to do all of those things is available. However, it is difficult to implement

Insider Notes: It is typically quite difficult for most customers to determine how to operate software products in a secure manner simply because vendors do not make it easy for them to understand how to do so. Asking vendors to simplify how to operate their software securely shouldn't be an unreasonable requirement since secure and safe operation is a given in most commercial products.

and comprehend. One of the main reasons for lack of network situational awareness is that the underpinnings of figuring out what is going on are not standardized. Specifically, there is no minimum standard for "auditability" and log files have no standard format.

For example, the 911 emergency phone number in the U.S. can handle cries for help in a few different languages, such as English and Spanish. However, if a call to 911 in New York City came in native Hawaiian, Homeric Greek or Aramaic, the chances of it being understood are slim. You can't figure out what is wrong, and how to help, if the communication is in multiple languages with few native speakers. Being able to do all of these things has got to be made easier. Not every problem of situational awareness would go away with standard logging, but unless parts of the network can speak the same language, it will be very hard to identify a problem in anything like real time.

The government has a heavy reliance on its IT networks. If the network can be brought down or, even worse, made to seem untrustworthy, it will be unable to accomplish its mission. The classic case of this occurred in the late 1960s when the U.S. deliberately had "bad code" put into controls systems for pipelines that were sold to the Soviet Union. It was designed to operate perfectly under test conditions but then to fail, ultimately causing a huge oil disaster. This caused the Russians to doubt the reliability of other systems they bought, as well. If bad actors infiltrated DOD and were able to corrupt information, it would make large parts of that data suspect and thus unreliable.

MARKET FAILURE — POOR SOFTWARE SECURITY

The fact that the quality of security in commercial software is not very good is a continuing market failure. This failure is arguably a public safety issue due to critical infrastructure's enormous reliance on an IT backbone. From the government standpoint, the poor quality and security-worthiness of commercial software fails to provide the security required for national security initiatives. From the general public safety perspective, almost all critical public infrastructure, such as telecommunications and financial services, rely on an IT backbone.

Unlike physical security, which is engineered to be safe, secure and reliable, IT products are not generally designed that way. A key reason for this lack of built-in security is inherent in how the industry and its products evolved and matured. Today, commercial software is designed for ultimate flexibility and adaptability to many different functions. Understanding the attraction of this flexibility to the market, vendors are reluctant to tell people exactly how to operate the application, often leaving it to the customer to determine how it can be best used within their environment. Also, software can generally do many things, depending on how it is configured (and what other software it is used with), unlike a bridge, which is not also designed to be an aircraft carrier or a helicopter, no matter how it is configured.

It is typically quite difficult for most customers to determine how to operate software products in a secure manner simply because vendors do not make it easy for them to understand how to do so. Asking vendors to simplify how to operate their software securely shouldn't be an unreasonable requirement since secure and safe operation is a given in most commercial products. For example, nobody drives a recently-purchased car off the lot and then discovers that they have to read the owner's manual to find the switch that makes the brakes work, or to make sure that the settings are correct so that the airbag will work. The safety mechanisms are in place and they work without owner intervention.

The absence of baseline security and "securability" is one of the fundamental problems with commercial software. It is generally difficult for customers to find out how to lock down an application. Vendors, as a group, do not make it easy for customers to understand how to do that. In fact, the guides on how to lock down a product, particularly one for large and complicated applications, tend to run into dozens, if not hundreds, of pages. If it is that complicated, how are customers going to be able to do it unless someone articulates it for them or gives them an automated tool?

Insider Notes: At a minimum, government should insist that the products it purchases be easy to lock down and easy to monitor. Locking products down into a secure condition should be a basic business practice, but it is not. Government pressure can be a force for this change.

CASE STUDY

TWO "LOCK DOWN" SCENARIOS

∎ **The USAF:** The Air Force had an enterprise software deal. One of the terms of their contract was that the vendor delivers its product in a locked-down configuration. They estimated that would save millions of dollars over the life of the contract. It also increased their security posture since they did not have to go in and tweak each application by hand. That is a big win.

A vendor that goes through all of the work to lock down their product for a big customer will most likely not jettison all of that work, but make it available to all customers. Therefore, the government has improved the security landscape of the entire sector at lower costs. When the vendor does the right thing at the beginning, it only has to be done once. A customer will have to do it for all iterations of its systems.

∎ **The DoE:** The Department of Energy (DoE) had an enterprise license agreement with a software developer. They told the vendor that they wanted them to make it easy to deploy their product securely within the enterprise. The DoE did not want to have to lock the thing down after it was installed. They asked the vendor to simplify the lock down process for them so that it would be easy to distribute the locked down version throughout their agency. The vendor worked with a third party to create scripts to lock down and distribute the secured version throughout the enterprise.

Because the customer was big and had an enterprise-wide license agreement, they could ask the vendor to work with them and help them to deploy the software securely. The DoE, the vendor and the third party were all pleased with the results.

The argument presented by vendors developing these applications is that customers do not ask for a locked down version. The lifecycle cost of securing products would be far lower if vendors do it once (document a baseline secure configuration, make it easy to install the product in that configuration and monitor the ongoing secure configuration), rather than having each customer do these steps separately.

Of course, even if one customer asks for a locked down version, this would not appear to the vendor as a groundswell requiring a revision in how they deliver product. However, if a very large customer segment with billions of dollars at stake makes this request, vendors will respond.

Another way to proceed is for government to take a more holistic approach and stop implementing these procurement criteria on an agency-by-agency basis. For example, it can state that the Department of Homeland Security has these procurement requirements for all of its software products. Or, it can have the Office of Management and Budget impose requirements that state that budget approval and funding will be tied to adherence to a specific policy. Since everyone that builds hardware or software products should be able to explain how to operate it securely, this would not be anti-competitive. At a minimum, government should insist that the products it purchases be easy to lock down and easy to monitor. Locking products down into a secure condition should be a basic business practice, but it is not. Government pressure can be a force for this change.

THREE ACTION ITEMS FOR VENDORS

One thing that government should do is to make it a procurement requirement for vendors to provide a product with a secure configuration. This involves requiring vendors to do three things:

- Document what a locked down configuration is so that customers know what it means.
- Make it easy to get there from here. The locked-down configuration should be the default, or customers should only need to either

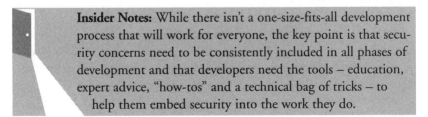

Insider Notes: While there isn't a one-size-fits-all development process that will work for everyone, the key point is that security concerns need to be consistently included in all phases of development and that developers need the tools – education, expert advice, "how-tos" and a technical bag of tricks – to help them embed security into the work they do.

A VENDOR THAT GOES THROUGH ALL OF THE WORK TO LOCK DOWN THEIR PRODUCT FOR A BIG CUSTOMER WILL MOST LIKELY NOT JETTISON ALL OF THAT WORK, BUT MAKE IT AVAILABLE TO ALL CUSTOMERS.

push a button on installation or activate a wizard. It should be easy to be made secure.

■ Include tools that can check security posture in the future, especially after patches and upgrades are implemented.

THE VENDORS' POSITION

After so many years of development, why does software continue to be so bad? It's primarily because of the success of the vendor development model. The standard model for software development was, and largely still is, to be first to market. In essence, the plan is: "Throw a product over the wall, grab market share, and worry about security and quality later." This model has been quite successful. Entire businesses have been successfully based on that model and have continued to thrive. However, companies are running their entire enterprises on software applications. In doing so, they are finding that the cost of the actual software is actually a small fraction of the cost of maintaining it over its life cycle. Hence, the true software cost is not in the licensing, but in maintenance and patching.

For example, let's say a worm hits a company's systems, due to a security fault, and now the company needs to buy antivirus software to defend itself. Why is this antivirus needed? Because there are big holes in the software that allow people to write worms and take advantage of those holes. Why is anti-spam needed? Because mail protocols to date have not done a very good job in filtering messages. The result is that most of these defensive products are band-aids (treating the symptom of bad security) instead of vaccines (curing the ailment). This added expense for defensive software is necessary even though most of these attacks are only possible because the base software that was initially bought was very poor.

There are a number of steps that vendors should take to ensure that security is baked-into their development processes. While there isn't a one-size-fits-all development process that will work for everyone, the key point is that security concerns need to be consistently included in all phases of development and that developers need the tools — education, expert advice, "how-tos" and a technical bag of tricks — to help them embed security into the work they do.

For example, having standards on secure coding practice (much of which is just good coding practice), with examples of good and bad code and "how tos," make it easier for developers to know how to avoid bad security practice and embrace good security practice. Training on general secure development practices, as well as more in-depth training (for example, in specific programming languages) is also helpful. Having standard security components is generally useful. For example, developers should not be writing their own cryptographic routines but should have access to standard, well-vetted FIPS-140 evaluated components. It is important to have a formalized development processes for which security is part of the requirements, design and testing. If security was not a consideration at the time a product, component or feature is being developed, it is typically very difficult to retrofit.

Testing can include the usual unit testing, integration testing and regression testing, but should also include destructive testing. In other words, exercising how a security feature is supposed to work is one thing; ensuring that code handles bad or malicious input gracefully is another. Automated security tools suitable for large independent software vendors are just becoming generally available on the market, and use of these can help automate checks for "bad code," or "badly-designed" code.

Testing also can include third party assessments, such as having a "blue team" of ethical hackers try to break the product (the team can be internal

Insider Notes: Government networks are now so large and complex, no agency has the capability to identify and understand what is happening on them. The government must insist that the commercial software industry provide it with the tools and capabilities to identify vulnerabilities and violations.

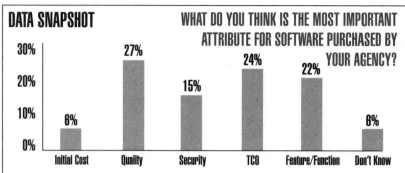

DATA SNAPSHOT — WHAT DO YOU THINK IS THE MOST IMPORTANT ATTRIBUTE FOR SOFTWARE PURCHASED BY YOUR AGENCY?

Initial Cost: 6%, Quality: 27%, Security: 15%, TCO: 24%, Feature/Function: 22%, Don't Know: 6%

Clearly, many *users* believe that the quality, security-worthiness and cost of ownership of software is very important. The question is, do the actual software *purchases* reflect those beliefs?

Download the complete research study for free at www.theblackbooks.com

Source: 2005 Larstan Business Reports

hackers, or a third party, or both). Similarly, products should be required to pass a series of checks prior to actual product shipment, whether the checks are self-administered or otherwise vetted (e.g., by a separate "development compliance" or "release management" team). Checks should include everything from secure configurations, so that products should be shipped or easily installable in an appropriately secure configuration, to ensuring that known, significant security vulnerabilities or weaknesses are addressed and checked off prior to product shipment.

No product is ever perfect, but responsible vendors need to ensure that products are designed and developed to be secure, and delivered securely, and that they do not knowingly put customers at unacceptable risk. Many vendors run their own companies on their own software, which should, in theory, make it easy for them to observe the Golden Rule of Software Security: Do unto others' IT systems as you would have done to your own. The stakes are all that much higher if you sell your product to the U.S. government, where "It's national security, stupid!"

GOVERNMENT CAN ADDRESS THIS FAILURE

The government buys billions of dollars worth of software, so their demands will be heard and it is in a very strong position to force change. The benefits of market change, pushed by the U.S. government as a Big

Buyer, will likely accrue to all sectors of critical infrastructure. Nobody will build good, quality software for the government and crappy, buggy software for the commercial market. The U.S. government also maintains networks that contain both state secrets and sensitive information about citizens of the U.S. and employees of government. Hence, the government *must* force their vendors to do the right thing. The government has two distinct options on how to do this.

It can always legislate change. This is especially applicable in a situation where a public safety issue has been ignored due to a market failure. It may be important to enforce standards for the public good. However, a core problem with legislation is that it has to be specific, measurable and enforceable to work. The benefits of the legislation should also exceed the cost. It is impossible to legislate "write better code" unless there is understanding of what "better" means, and "better" can be measured. More specificity around "better" is important so vendors (and ultimately, developers) know whether they are in or out of compliance. And some metric or methods around "write better code" is required, or this will be difficult to measure. Also, legislation tends to be relatively inflexible compared to procurement vehicles.

The second option is to use the procurement power the government has in abundance to require better behavior and better security from their vendors. In addition to the fact that we've seen that procurement can work, as discussed earlier, nobody can argue that procurement is anti-competitive or unfair to some vendors: after all, a large customer with critical security needs that spends billions of dollars on software *should* "get what they pay for," correct? Furthermore, "Big Buyer" procurement power tends to be more flexible than "Big Brother" legislation or regulation, which means

Insider Notes: A software product should be scanned for security faults with a good tool and be tested to ensure that it does what it is suppose to do. For example, you can have a secure door built from good wood, but it doesn't have a lock on it because it wasn't designed to have a lock on it. The result is a really good door that doesn't do what doors are supposed to do.

THE BENEFITS OF MARKET CHANGE, PUSHED BY THE U.S. GOVERNMENT AS A BIG BUYER, WILL LIKELY ACCRUE TO ALL SECTORS OF CRITICAL INFRASTRUCTURE.

that the tool of procurement power is adaptable and flexible, depending on what kind of software is being bought, by whom and for what purpose.

THE COMMON CRITERIA

Even in the absence of a direct public good issue, government has an interest in understanding how the commercial software that it buys is developed. Government networks are now so large and complex, no agency has the capability to identify and understand what is happening on them. The government must insist that the commercial software industry provide it with the tools and capabilities to identify vulnerabilities and violations. Creating broad standards for software capability can fulfill this need, or the government can wield its purchasing power. This purchasing power can be used to hold vendors accountable for delivering products with a higher standard of security. One way for government to accomplish this is to require outside validation of products to ensure that they are security worthy, like the international Common Criteria (ISO-15408).

Ultimately, the only way that government will be able to get what it wants is to make it a procurement requirement. When using procurement power, it can enforce uniformity of quality and give itself choices. The government could raise the floor for industry — and the ceiling, too. This is the difference between building a better house, and creating better building codes.

A fear is that the government could define a procurement requirement so strictly that it is effectively a sole source contract. For example, it could say that it will only buy relational databases that have functions XYZ that only one company can provide. This would not be particularly competitive. It would not result in good prices and enough choices. What government needs to do is clearly state that it insists that all companies do a better job in building software and it wants everyone to show that they validate their products through independent measures, such as against the Common Criteria.

Common Criteria addresses one part of the software issue, vetting claims. In other words, what is this product intended to do in security? How well, in fact, does it do that, and how comfortable are the evaluators that the product does what it says it does in security?

The Common Criteria, can but generally does not, address the other part of the equation, which is if the product is free, or largely free, of unintended defects that could lead to security problems. The so-called "vulnerability assessment" part of security evaluations generally is not done for commercial software to any great degree. What's needed is either a secondary vetting process to test for vulnerabilities, or vulnerability assessments completed at lower assurance levels as part of Common Criteria evaluations.

Checking that a product doesn't have security faults buys some security but says nothing about whether the product protects against the threats it is supposed to protect against. For example, there can be a perfectly working lock on a "really secure" door, but the door might have a doggie door embedded in it. It was designed to protect against human threats but not against small humans crawling through doggie doors.

By insisting on this process, government will raise the bar for software capability in a consistent manner that is not inherently uncompetitive, and give itself some selection among products with similar capability. As a byproduct, it can wind up raising the bar for industry.

The Common Criteria is not a perfect vehicle, but at least it provides some commonality for identifying what threats the product will encounter and how well it will respond to them. This can be considered as a first phase in determining product quality. This process can also be applied to demonstrat-

Insider Notes: One thing that government must ask for in a product procurement requirement is documentation on how the product was built. This documentation should identify how the product was developed, identify if the company has some methodology for building the application and define that methodology.

ing that the product is free of unintended consequences. This can be accomplished by requiring a code scan or automated vulnerability assessment.

A software product should be scanned for security faults with a good tool and be tested to ensure that it does what it is suppose to do. For example, you can have a secure door built from good wood, but it doesn't have a lock on it because it wasn't designed to have a lock on it. The result is a really good door that doesn't do what doors are supposed to do. In software evaluation, you need to assess both what the product was intended to do and how well it actually does it.

The Common Criteria is a good thing because, all other things being equal within a reasonable assurance level, it forces companies to build their product better. It requires vendors to have functional and design documentation and to conduct valid security tests. In simply insisting on the use of evaluated products, even if in a proscribed class of usage, the government can change how products are built, and embed security into product development processes. A vendor building security into a product during the development process is superior to waiting until two weeks prior to shipping product before determining that security was forgotten and then trying to bolt it on.

More products are now required to go through this evaluation simply because the government has indicated that it is serious about only accepting product that meets this criteria (e.g., for classified systems, as required by National Security Telecommunications and Information Security Policy [NSTISSP] #11, and its DOD interpretation, DOD 8500.1). This has had the effect of altering the perception of security evaluations from that of an expensive check box, to that of a forum for the industry to discuss what is working, what is good and how it can be made better. Evaluations can become something that raises the bar for software assurance without, ideally, becoming a barrier to entry.

STANDARDS ALSO GET THE JOB DONE

Government can also enforce technical standards where there is a large and important public issue that obviously won't be corrected by market forces. Creating and implementing standards and wielding purchasing power are certainly not the same thing, but they are related in terms of how they can improve the quality of software. For example, government may not specify a standard way to lock products down, but it could state that it is a procurement requirement for vendors to provide one secure configuration, available out-of-the-box, when delivering commercial software. The government has some precedent in this by insisting, on at least one occasion, that a vendor deliver a product in a locked-down configuration. By doing so, it saved millions of dollars over the life of the contract and substantially raised security. As a side benefit, once a vendor locks its product down and delivers it to the government, it is highly likely that it will do the same thing for its commercial customers. Vendors will most likely not deliver a locked version to the government and a wide-open, "EZ Hack" version to other customers.

The government can and has set system-wide requirements for all of its agencies. Setting requirements, however, does not always mean that they are followed. The government had a security evaluation requirement for products purchased for the DOD (evaluation against the old Orange Book) but the requirement for evaluated products was never enforced consistently, until relatively recently. In the past, the DOD ostensibly encouraged vendors to invest millions of dollars to complete and comply with security evaluations (against the Orange Book), and then would buy whatever it wanted off-the-shelf, whether or not it was evaluated. Finally, Congress legislated that the DOD had to follow its own policies. Now, most vendors selling software products to the DOD that will be used in classified systems have their software evaluated. The salient point is that if security is embedded in a procurement requirement that has teeth and allows no waivers, vendors will comply.

Insider Notes: At some point in the future, when there are enough tools that are available, affordable and proven to work properly, then proof of scanning should be a procurement requirement. This should help alleviate one of the biggest unbudgeted software expenses incurred by customers – a large amount of required software maintenance and patches.

GOVERNMENT CAN ALSO ENFORCE TECHNICAL STANDARDS WHERE THERE IS A LARGE AND IMPORTANT PUBLIC ISSUE THAT OBVIOUSLY WON'T BE CORRECTED BY MARKET FORCES.

Government enforcement of procurement standards (e.g., regarding NSTISSP #11 and DOD 8500.1) has already resulted in more products being evaluated prior to purchase. The fact that government is currently in discussions with the vendor community on how they can both help improve the assurance of commercial software (including the Common Criteria, but not limited to the use of the Common Criteria) is an encouraging sign.

RAISING THE BAR

One thing that government must ask for in a product procurement requirement is documentation on how the product was built. This documentation should identify how the product was developed, identify if the company has some methodology for building the application and define that methodology. The government's goal for this requirement should be to foster a common body of knowledge of what is good development practice. Automatic detection and remediation of security vulnerabilities prior to products shipping should be an integral part of that process. For certain classes of product, a procurement requirement should include that the vendor demonstrate that some type of code scanning tool was utilized in the development process. This would ensure that this product is free of major quality and security defects.

Now emerging is a set of tools that will scan an application and indicate whether there are defects in the code. Currently, the utility of these tools is limited by their penchant for raising false alarms (so-called false positives). At some point in the future, when there are enough tools that are available, affordable and proven to work properly, then proof of scanning should be a procurement requirement. This should help alleviate one of the biggest unbudgeted software expenses incurred by customers — a large amount of required software maintenance and patches.

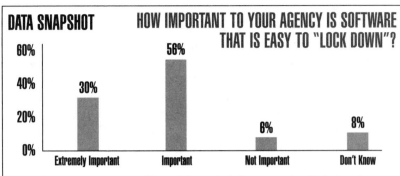

DATA SNAPSHOT

HOW IMPORTANT TO YOUR AGENCY IS SOFTWARE THAT IS EASY TO "LOCK DOWN"?

Given the strong importance of "easy ability to lock down a product," it's clear that support for a "default secure" installation should be a standard U.S. government procurement requirement.

Download the complete research study for free at www.theblackbooks.com

Source: 2005 Larstan Business Reports

These expenses can't be budgeted and are therefore ruinous to budgets, especially government budgets, since they tend to be bigger and have so many more installations of a given product. The optimal source code vulnerability assessment tool needs to be flexible enough to meet the demands of different vendors, and they must reach a wide range of requirements. Good coding practice and avoidance of common security faults is something all vendors need to comply with, no matter what their size or market segment.

THE LACK OF AUDITING CAPABILITY

Auditing, in particular, is not a sexy part of security, albeit a basic part. When people do talk about security, they talk about confidentiality, integrity and availability/accountability. Companies don't base their purchasing decision on a product's auditing capability. They might be concerned about whether it can do encryption on the Web because of confi-

Insider Notes: Without government action, "critical infrastructure" – e.g., a transcontinental railroad – would never have been built. The need for situational awareness on all networks, which requires a common audit format and common auditability standards, is a key component for securing everyone's IT infrastructure, especially the government's.

dentiality concerns. However, auditing has never been that critical a concern. The one thing that seems to be changing this position is compliance requirements. Agencies now have to keep records on and track who did what with their information, as well as who granted what privileges to whom. There is currently no minimal standard for what is an acceptable level of audit capability or for minimally acceptable audit functionality. There are certainly no widely adopted auditing formats. This lack of a common standard for auditing is partly the result of a lack of a forcing function.

Audit is a tactical, feature/function area where the government can force needed change on industry. For example, NIST could develop a standard for audit, vet it by industry and get industry input, do a reference implementation if applicable and have it eventually become a standard purchasing requirement. One example of how government achieved this was with the transcontinental railroad. Prior to this railroad being built, there was no standard train gauge. Every railroad had a different gauge so the tracks did not interoperate. The government wanted to build a transcontinental railroad and forced the train gauge to be a standard 4' 8 1/2". If it hadn't, the trains would still all be local and of various gauges. Only Uncle Sam was big enough to force that change upon industry, for the public good.

Without government action, "critical infrastructure" — e.g., a transcontinental railroad — would never have been built. The need for situational awareness on all networks, which requires a common audit format and common auditability standards, is a key component for securing everyone's IT infrastructure, especially the government's.

GOVERNMENT IS BEGINNING TO IMPOSE ITS WILL

The government is getting somewhat smarter. Most requests for proposals (RFPs) now ask if risk assessment has been conducted on the software and/or whether anyone outside the company validated it. Consequently, there is a gradual realization of the need for better software, but it is not widespread or well organized. The generally poor quality of commercial software is a national security issue since the entire infrastructure relies on an IT backbone. The government should be taking the lead in best development practice definitions. This can be part of a certification process.

However, the bottom line is that there needs to be a revolution in the software industry. Many of the movers and shakers in this industry are not forward thinking enough to perceive and understand what is at stake here. They still see product development and product quality as simply a business issue responding to revenue and profit, not as a national security issue. They must step up and accept accountability, to help ensure the safety of the entire nation. Government must provide this incentive.

Commercial software has entered a new arena where its flaws and vulnerabilities are no longer inconsequential. The existing policy model of fixing bad software later with maintenance and patching is no longer acceptable. Software vulnerabilities can now put key government infrastructures at risk and even impact battlefield results. Therefore, the government must apply its weight as a huge market for commercial software as a "forcing function," to insist on security improvements and consistent quality.

■ ■ ■

Mary Ann Davidson is the Chief Security Officer at Oracle Corporation, responsible for Oracle product security, as well as security evaluations, assessments and incident handling. She represents Oracle on the Board of Directors of the Information Technology Information Security Analysis Center (IT-ISAC). She was recently named one of Information Security's top five "Women of Vision" and is a 2004 Fed100 award recipient from Federal Computer Week. She has also participated in multiple advisory groups to the U.S. Federal government related to software assurance.

Ms. Davidson has a B.S.M.E. from the University of Virginia and a M.B.A. from the Wharton School of the University of Pennsylvania. She has also served as a commissioned officer in the U.S. Navy Civil Engineer Corps, during which she was awarded the Navy Achievement Medal. She can be reached at 650-506-5464 or mary.ann.davidson@oracle.com.

[4]
STANDARDS:
THE NEXT BIG STEPS

Government security standards are continually evolving. Standards, of course, are the "Holy Grail" of any government IT system, but achieving comprehensive, end-to-end security is no simple matter. That's especially true in the realm of Next Generation Network (NGN) security, where a cohesive architecture is needed to deploy end-to-end network solutions. Here's a closer look at the constantly changing nature of this nettlesome problem and practical ways to address it.

> "JUST AS IN NATURE SYSTEMS OF ORDER GOVERN THE GROWTH AND STRUCTURE OF ANIMATE AND INANIMATE MATTER, SO HUMAN ACTIVITY ITSELF HAS, SINCE THE EARLIEST TIMES, BEEN DISTINGUISHED BY THE QUEST FOR ORDER."
> — Josef Muller-Brockmann, famed graphic designer

by S. RAO VASIREDDY

Everyone agrees that standards are necessary to add efficiency and rationality to information systems. Taking this view is akin to embracing mom and apple pie: few will argue that they're laudable values. But when the time comes to pick specific standards and apply them in the network lifecycle, well, that's when consensus becomes elusive.

THERE ARE MANY EXISTING STANDARDS TODAY. DO THEY PROVIDE AN ARCHITECTURE FRAMEWORK TO GUIDE A CIO TO PLAN, IMPLEMENT AND OPERATE NETWORKS SECURELY?

A CIO of a government agency must consider various standards and guidelines and then apply the relevant aspects needed to secure the agency's IT network. Today there is a myriad of government standards and guidelines in the area of information security. These standards provide specific security recommendations for numerous systems, applications and processes. However, they do not provide a unified and comprehensive security architecture framework that is necessary to plan, design and implement end-to-end network security.

There is a need for an overarching standards framework which can function as a guide to identify potential security gaps, in a comprehensive manner, for design, implementation and maintenance phases of the security life cycle. Currently, specific standards developed for network elements, algorithms and process guidelines are helpful within given areas of security.

These standards are developed by various organizations such as National Institute of Standards and Technology (NIST), Defense Information Systems Agency (DISA), National Security Agency (NSA), etc. Encryption, for example, has many detailed standards including design and certification criteria as presented in Federal Information Processing Standards (FIPS).

While FIPS standards are well established guidelines for the design and implementation of encryption, how do they fit into securing an end-to-end network? If a CIO in a government agency follows FIPS, Federal Enterprise Architecture (FEA) guidelines and other select NIST standards, will it be sufficient to ensure comprehensive end-to-end network security? What else is needed to ensure secure planning, design and maintenance of networks?

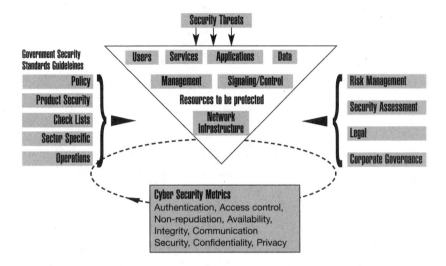

FIGURE 1: CURRENT STATE OF SECURITY STANDARDS

Figure 1 is a pictorial depiction of how security standards and best practices contribute to security.

What's needed is an architecture framework that cohesively leverages the strengths of these standards. To be useful, any new security standards framework should be consistent with the evolving nature of security, and must address the emerging paradigm shift occurring in security caused by the convergence of networks and applications. It also needs to complement existing standards and illustrate how to analyze and implement security more efficiently.

Insider Notes: To be useful, any new security standards framework should be consistent with the evolving nature of security, and must address the emerging paradigm shift occurring in security caused by the convergence of networks and applications. It also needs to complement existing standards and illustrate how to analyze and implement security more efficiently.

DATA SNAPSHOT

Can you identify the network security perimeters in a converged boundless network which uses multiple environments such as wireless, wireline and IP?

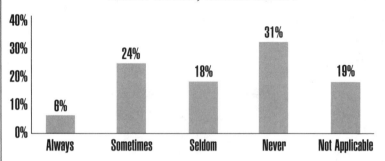

Security perimeters are dynamic in the Next Generation Networks (NGN) that support converged voice, data and multimedia applications. A good security architecture framework should enable an engineer to analyze the NGN environment in a holistic way to implement end-to-end security even with the elastic security perimeters.

Download the complete research study for free at www.theblackbooks.com

Source: 2005 Larstan Business Reports

THE FEDERAL GOVERNMENT PERSPECTIVE

The Federal Information Security Management Act of 2002 (FISMA) provides a charter to the Office of Management and Budget (OMB) to evaluate security within government agencies. The FISMA Act assigns specific responsibilities to federal agencies, the National Institute of Standards and Technology (NIST) and the Office of Management and Budget (OMB), to strengthen information system security. This act defines security as protecting information and information systems from unauthorized access, use, disclosure, destruction, modification or destruction, to provide comprehensive security. The purpose of this act is to define and enforce requirements that ensure that government systems are safe, secure and available, and that the networks and the information within them are not modified.

There are several security standards that can be used to help implement the directives defined in FISMA. FISMA requires the head of each agency to implement policies and procedures to reduce information technology security risks in a cost effective manner. FISMA also requires agency CIOs to conduct annual reviews of their information security program and report the results to OMB.

Since 2002, much has happened in the manner in which networks are implemented and applications share the networks. The phone is no longer a dumb device. It is evolving into an intelligence device, and it will not be too long before these devices are as powerful as PCs. Wireless, wireline data and voice networks are converging and increasingly use shared TCP/IP infrastructure. Therefore, while the intent of FISMA is still valid and remains effective, the landscape, which it was developed to address, is continually changing. The convergence of networks and applications, and the use of open platforms give rise to new security concerns and threats, which calls for a reinterpretation and augmentation of the definition for end-to-end security.

THE CHANGING NATURE OF NETWORKS

The architecture, usage and technologies of networks have changed substantially. Back in the 70s and 80s, there were two different networked worlds, one for voice communications and the other for data communications. Circuit switched voice networks were mostly used for speech applications and for low speed data applications, such as dial-up data and fax traffic. Data traffic was secondary to voice services, and it was easy to differentiate what was a voice network and what was a data network.

Insider Notes: Networks have become extremely complex, and loss due to attacks increases as security vulnerabilities are exposed to security threats, even when the intruder doesn't have malicious intent of causing damage. Security management is also much more complex than simply maintaining authentication or access control. The growing complexity and convergence of the voice and data applications should be a key factor in driving the evolution of security standards.

THE LATEST FBI REPORT PUBLISHED IN 2005 FOUND THAT ATTACK FREQUENCY ON THE NETWORK IS NEARLY EQUAL BETWEEN OUTSIDERS AND INSIDERS.

At that time, people were not overly concerned about security even though those networks were certainly not totally secure. Voice networks were wired to a switch and traffic was not generally encrypted. Still, there was a perception of privacy and security because it was not easy to hack into a phone call. In the data world, communication was initially accomplished through LANs or dedicated data lines, and eventually through WAN, Packet (X.25, FR) and ATM technologies.

From the dedicated datalines, data communications moved to "layer two" data networks that allowed sharing of WAN bandwidth. These networks still provided secure access. To hack into a data network at that time required a complex set of resources and skill levels that were very difficult to acquire.

Today, there is a general acceptance and use of the Internet, in addition to the wide use of PCs. Networks are now more IP based, with interfaces to multiple networks. Voice, data and wireless networks are converging and are interdependent on one another to provide the users with required services and applications. This is a fundamental change; the networks are not dedicated to a specific type of traffic, but most of the time they share network infrastructure to support many different voice and data applications.

Both private and government organizations use or interface with the public data networks. This has expanded the area of a security perimeter from clearly identifiable boundaries to a wider network that sometimes includes the Internet. The network, which was previously not very well known, is now open in many ways in which security administrators need to be conscious. For example, management systems can be accessed through the Internet and security attacks can originate from insiders as well as outsiders.

The latest FBI report published in 2005 found that attack frequency on the network is nearly equal between outsiders and insiders. According to these statistics, outsiders and insiders accounted for 47 percent and 53 percent, respectively, of security attacks on the networks. These numbers have been more or less the same over recent years. This data indicates that the networks have become extremely complex, and loss due to attacks increases as security vulnerabilities are exposed to security threats, even when the intruder doesn't have malicious intent of causing damage. Security management is also much more complex than simply maintaining authentication or access control. The growing complexity and convergence of the voice and data applications should be a key factor in driving the evolution of security standards.

Intelligence and flexibility of use and the ability to move from one network to another define the current information age. Fifteen years ago, major service providers were planning and touting "Anytime-Anywhere Communications." Now the "anytime-anywhere" communication vision is not only a reality, but also NGN services allow portability of voice, data and multimedia applications. Network functionality is also evolving to offer flexible management and provisioning. Service and application management can be done centrally by a network provider or locally by the end-user in many cases.

There are also different applications that use different control protocols. These control protocols are part and parcel of the network elements and end-devices. The tight coupling between applications and end-user devices will slowly disappear. The application control/signaling protocols available

Insider Notes: A CIO of a government agency today may allow several types of networks, but not WiFi, because this technology is not considered secure. However, it will not be long before WiFi and other wireless technologies are widely used in government agencies due to productivity gains and new applications that need to be supported. A security framework that applies to networks independent of technology is desirable to ensure uniform levels of security implementation.

SECURITY BOUNDARIES OF A NETWORK ARE NOT STATIC, BUT ELASTIC. THEY VARY, WITH SERVICES AND APPLICATIONS SUPPORTED AT ANY GIVEN MOMENT.

at the end-user devices provide new avenues of security attack to hackers. Security now needs to be thought through on many realms. It is not just about a network element or user-data anymore, but must be considered from an end-to-end perspective.

NETWORKS WITHOUT BOUNDARIES

Security discussions have usually been conducted within certain types of boundary definitions. These boundaries have traditionally been confined to pre-defined interfaces. This is not the case anymore as described in the section above. Physical boundaries have begun to disappear with logical boundaries assuming their place. Logical boundaries are not static and they vary as a function of time, place and application.

Time and place will determine what type (3G, WiFi, wireline, public, private) of networks and what kind (wireless, wireline) of interfaces will be preferable to the end-users. In a converged IP/voice network and NGN service environment, the security perimeters will be quite dynamic. When an application is accessed from a remote location using the Internet, the security should be designed to protect the entry of attacks from the Internet and also maintain the sanctity of end-point security. This would require more than a security design for authentication and encryption.

There are intelligent end-user devices, which support many applications and require same degree of security functionality in different networks. Security interoperability is the key to enable operations of the applications in the office, at home or in the car making the network boundaries more flexible.

A CIO of a government agency today may allow several types of networks, but not WiFi, because this technology is not considered secure. However, it will not be long before WiFi and other wireless technologies are widely used in government agencies due to productivity gains and new applications that need to be supported. A security framework that applies to networks independent of technology is desirable to ensure uniform levels of security implementation.

QUALITY OF SECURITY: A NEW PARADIGM

Current security frameworks and standards lack an approach to analyze quality of security. Any new security framework should help in the end-to-end planning, design and maintenance of the security of NGN networks while complementing the current standards. The goal is to establish a methodology to determine quality of security. For example, if very strong encryption is required, can the application tolerate the accompanying delays in processing? If the answer is yes, what are the other metrics required to assess quality of security?

The quality of security is a new paradigm that is not well addressed in today's security standards. Many of the current security frameworks combine more granular security metrics into availability, integrity and confidentially. This view needs to be expanded to develop the necessary additional security metrics. When these metrics are expanded and incorporated into a comprehensive security framework, a quality of security definition similar to the network Quality of Service (QoS) measures of throughput and propagation delay will be achievable.

When the list of security metrics is expanded, it becomes apparent that current network security measurement concepts are not adequate. For

Insider Notes: A framework for standards evolution needs to consider end-to-end security in multiple aspects of network operation, such as user data, signaling, management, traffic between different elements, traffic between different users and so on. When defining a security standard, each asset in the network that needs to be protected must be reviewed in terms of all of the security dimensions, security planes and security layers that are relevant.

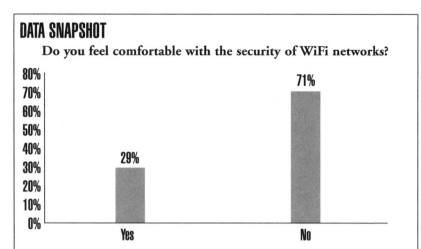

DATA SNAPSHOT

Do you feel comfortable with the security of WiFi networks?

WiFi security is not well understood and the design, implementation and operations of security for WiFi is complex. A well thought out security architecture framework, together with the WiFi security standards are essential to increase WiFi footprint, in government enterprise space, and leverage the advantages of WiFi technology.

Download the complete research study for free at www.theblackbooks.com
Source: 2005 Larstan Business Reports

example, almost everyone understands availability. A dial tone is a common characteristic indicating availability of PSTN phone service. However, a VoIP call doesn't need a dial tone to work. A hacker on a data network can launch a Denial of Service attack on a specific VoIP end-device or phone, without impacting the network's ability to process the call. To comprehensively characterize how the hacker from a data network impacts end-to-end VoIP service availability, one needs to know the security interactions of management, control and user traffic and its impact on networks, services and applications.

Even the well understood "availability" measure no longer depends just on one security dimension but is interrelated with other security metrics, which impact different types of network traffic differently. The security architecture frameworks need to evolve, to ensure that gaps can be easily identified and the relevant, existing technical standards are leveraged to establish and maintain end-to-end "quality" of security.

TAKING SECURITY TO THE NEXT LEVEL

To take the security definition to the next level, it needs to be defined in finer detail and take into account the paradigm shift occurring in today's world. For example, take national security. Hurricane Katrina caused extensive loss of communications. In the future, emergency responders may carry intelligent devices that are operational even during unexpected emergencies, by having redundant access, automated switch over to operational networks, etc. Therefore, communication would always be available regardless of whether the switch or cell site is down. They could have a network that will work at all times and be able to download maps and show locations where help is most needed. Security is a key aspect that needs to be implemented by design to achieve such a vision.

Another example is the evolution of technology in health care where information can be transferred in real time from a remote location to the hospital, to allow the doctor a wider window of time to respond. To do this, a new vision of security is needed to ensure the accurate and timely delivery of information without violating HIPPA regulations. Such an implementation needs to view the network and its security in multiple dimensions on an end-to-end basis, not a box-to-box or protocol-to-protocol basis. The need is to start at a high level and leverage the detailed network element/protocol level security standards. How can security be managed? Is security required in terms of routing and application context? Or does it vary by the network interaction with different types of networks and the mobility between the network and different users and applications?

Insider Notes: A major gap in standards today is that the framework and standards that are defined are technology or systems or sector specific. The disjoint standards can be leveraged if a framework can divide the target network into granular aspects of security. The different security planes, layers and dimensions of the X.805 framework provide the security engineer an avenue to design and implement the networks with the required degree of security.

SUPPORTING THE PARADIGM SHIFT

ITU-T X.805 (ISO 18028-2) provides a security architecture framework to dissect the end-to-end security planning, implementation and maintenance into easily manageable segments that help address the issues described in previous sections of this document.

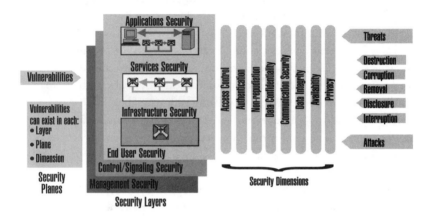

FIGURE 2: SECURITY ARCHITECTURE FOR END-TO-END COMMUNICATIONS

This diagram illustrates the various aspects of security. It encompasses substantively more than just the availability, integrity and confidentiality of one network element or certain types of data.

The diagram presents a three dimensional architectural framework of network security by using security layers, security planes and security dimensions. The following three security planes identify specific areas within the network:

❶ Management security
❷ Control / signature security
❸ End-user security

The following three security layers identify specific elements of a network:

❶ Application security
❷ Services security
❸ Infrastructure security

NETWORK QUALITY, AVAILABILITY AND RELIABILITY ARE TIGHTLY COUPLED WITH SECURITY DUE TO CONVERGENCE AND USE OF OPEN PLATFORMS AND OPERATING SYSTEMS. A GRANULAR DEFINITION OF SECURITY METRICS IS REQUIRED TO ESTABLISH AND TRACK THE QUALITY OF SECURITY.

Combined, these security plans and security layers create a three-by-three matrix with nine plane/layer-defined cells. For example, within management security there is an application security component, a services security component and an infrastructure security component. The same is the case for the other security planes.

There are also eight security dimensions that describe specific types of security implementations. These are defined as:

❶ **Access Control:** The main purpose is to protect the resource from unauthorized use. A resource can be software, a network element and a service, as well as other items. It protects these resources from unauthorized use. Firewalls are an example of access control. Access control protects against unauthorized use of network resources. It ensures that only authorized personnel or devices are allowed access to network elements, stored information, information flows, services and applications. In addition, different privilege levels guarantee that individuals and devices can only gain access to and perform operations on the network elements, stored information and information flows for which they are authorized.

❷ **Authentication:** Authentication is used to confirm the identities of communicating entities. Authentication ensures the validity of the claimed identities of the entities participating in the communication (e.g., person, device, service or application). Passwords are an example. Passwords can be between people and machines or between two different devices. It can be between processes. There are more complex and stronger means to authentication than password, such as biometrics, two-factor authentication or stronger password. Depending on the criticality of the resource being protected, there are different levels and different layers of authentication that need to be implemented.

❸ **Non-Repudiation:** Non-repudiation provides proof of the origin of data or the cause of an event or an action. It ensures the creation of evidence that can be used to prove that an event or action has taken place so that the cause of the event or action cannot be repudiated later. It provides evidence that can be used to prove that some event or action took place and cannot be denied.

❹ **Data Confidentiality:** Data confidentiality protects data from unauthorized disclosure. Data confidentiality ensures that data is kept private from unauthorized access or viewing. Encryption, coupled with access management techniques, is often used to keep data secure.

❺ **Communications security:** Communications security ensures that information flows only between the authorized endpoints and that the information flow is not diverted or intercepted as it flows between these endpoints. Communication security is critical because of the use of the Internet and converged networks.

❻ **Data Integrity:** Data integrity ensures the correctness or accuracy of data against unauthorized modification, deletion, creation and replication and provides an indication of unauthorized activities in these areas. The data integrity security dimension addresses the modification and fabrication security threats.

❼ **Availability:** Availability ensures that there is no denial of authorized access to network elements, stored information, information flows, services and applications due to events impacting the network. Disaster recovery solutions are included in this category. A valid user should not be denied access to a network element, stored information, service or application.

❽ **Privacy:** Privacy provides protection of information that might be derived from the observation of network activities. This dimension also includes protection of information associated with individual users, service providers, enterprises or the network infrastructure that might be obtained either by direct or covert means. Examples of this information include Web sites that a user has visited, a user's geographic location and the IP addresses and DNS names of devices in a service provider network.

Each of the eight security dimensions applies to the three security planes and three security layers, depending on the object and the degree of specific threat.

SECURITY: A MULTI-DIMENSIONAL PROBLEM

	Infrastructure Layer	Services Layer	Applications Layer
Management Plane	Module One	Module Four	Module Seven
Control/Signaling Plane	Module Two	Module Five	Module Eight
User Plane	Module Three	Module Six	Module Nine

Execute
- Management Network: Top Row
- Network Services: Middle Column
- Security Module: Layer & Plane Intersection

Access Control	Communication Security
Authentication	Data Integrity
Non-Repudiation	Availability
Data Confidentiality	Privacy

The 8 Security Dimensions Are Applied to Each Security Module

FIGURE 3: MULTIPLE-DIMENSIONS OF SECURITY

The above diagram depicts the matrix defined by the three security planes and three security levels. Each of the cells defined by the matrix needs to be properly designed, implemented and maintained. This presents a multi-dimensional problem. With the paradigm shift, security is defined with boundaries that change depending on the application and objective. Security can't be addressed in simplistic terms; it must be defined multi-dimensionally across the life cycle of both the network and the enterprise. This needs to be done upfront when the service is defined.

There are three different phases of security:
1. Planning and definition
2. Designing and implementation
3. Operations and maintenance

A framework for standards evolution needs to consider end-to-end security in multiple aspects of network operation such as user data, signaling, management, traffic between different elements, traffic between different users

DATA SNAPSHOT

Are you aware of any security standard for planning, implementing and maintaining end-to-end security?

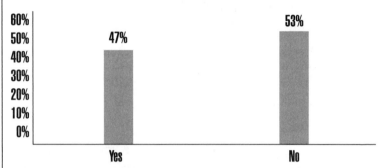

Government enterprise networks can make use of a security framework such as ITU-T X.805 / ISO 18028-2 to plan, implement and maintain end-to-end security. X.805 framework will complement other government security standards (FEA, FIPS, NIST) to strengthen enterprise security.

Download the complete research study for free at www.theblackbooks.com
Source: 2005 Larstan Business Reports

and so on. The framework defined above is flexible enough to be used as a guideline for evolving security standards.

When defining a security standard, each asset in the network that needs to be protected must be reviewed in terms of all of the security dimensions, security planes and security layers that are relevant.

HOW THE NEW FRAMEWORK HELPS

Take the case of WiFi in government agencies. There are many security recommendations for WiFi, such as NIST 800-48. However, it is focused on enterprise WiFi networks and does not include IP networks or security interoperability with 3G mobile networks. This standard can be used along with other established guidelines for firewalls, IP network security and other recommendations on monitoring and auditing networks. However, even with all these standards together, a network engineer can't be certain that end-to-end security has been achieved for all different phases of the life-cycle from design and planning to implementation maintenance.

A framework such as X.805 will be invaluable in developing such a view, since it can be used to verify if the design and implementation has taken into consideration the more granular security dimensions in multiple security layers and security planes. When an agency is designing a new network or deploying a new technology such as WiFi, they can utilize X.805 framework to analyze security aspects of solutions provided by their vendors. The eight security dimensions across the different planes and layers can be applied by government agencies to verify that a solution provides comprehensive, end-to-end security independent of new technologies utilized in the networks.

A major gap in standards today is that the framework and standards that are defined are technology or systems or sector specific. The disjoint standards can be leveraged if a framework can divide the target network into granular aspects of security. The different security planes, layers and dimensions of the X.805 framework provide the security engineer an avenue to design and implement the networks with the required degree of security.

WiFi TAKES FLIGHT

WiFi has become very popular not only in the private enterprise space and in public hotspots, but also in some government agencies. If somebody is looking for mobility within the local enterprise environment, WiFi pro-

Insider Notes: Implementation must avoid solely depending on the domain knowledge of the IT staff for the correct design and deployment of network security. When a new technology (e.g., WiFi) is introduced in a government network, the CIO should employ a security framework such as X.805. Applying the X.805 framework and verifying that applicable security dimensions are addressed in different security planes and security layers in the project definition, design and maintenance phases, would help to implement end-to-end security requirements.

WiFi: THE GAO GETS GOING

(This case study is based on GAO Report to House of Reps 5/2005: "Information Security and the Need to Improve Controls on Wireless networks. Report Number GAO-G05-383.")

Commonly available WiFi detection equipment is not very expensive and can be purchased off the shelf. This equipment scans for WiFi networks and includes a tool to gain access to them. Driving around a neighborhood with a PC that's loaded with this detection gear can detect a WiFi signal. Once found, it can probe the network for easy access and exploit security vulnerabilities.

GAO took this WiFi detection equipment and rode around Washington, DC looking to detect two different types of networks. The first were the WiFi networks controlled and deployed by a government agency. These agencies should have monitored and managed their wireless access points. The second were ad hoc networks where people working within an agency created an obviously unsecured network on their own using a laptop.

While cruising a 15 square block area of the nation's capital with this WiFi scanner, the GAO detected several wireless networks operating within the networks of federal agencies. They discovered signal leaks and identified that the networks were not secure. A properly designed WiFi network configures the strength of the radio signal so that access can be confined to the premises. However, avoiding signal leak may not always be feasible. If this signal leaks to the parking lot, the agency has now lost control of its network security since the parking lot is accessible to the general public. Signal leakage is especially worrisome if the building is right next to a street, a highway or a fast food restaurant.

A WiFi signal can typically broadcast from 150 feet to 1500 feet. If the range is too short, then the WiFi coverage inside the building is insufficient. That is the trade off. Just because there may be all federal agencies in one area doesn't mean that the signal from one agency building should "leak" into that of another building, since each agency is responsible for its own security. What GAO discovered was that these agencies often lacked the controls and policies, such as detailed guidelines on how to design and configure the end points and train employees not to form ad hoc networks, which are necessary to secure wireless networks.

The most salient specific results:

- ■ Signal leakage was detected outside six headquarters of federal agencies.
- ■ Ad hoc networks could be detected at all six agencies.
- ■ Many agencies reported that they did not have documented security requirements for wireless networks.
- ■ Most agencies do not have a comprehensive security-monitoring plan.

Detecting rogue networks is not rocket science. Network security and intrusion detection systems are available on the WiFi side as well as on the wired LAN side. The WiFi access point site can be configured to detect unauthorized networks. Still, only six of 15 agencies monitored the facilities continuously. The rest did it "periodically," which could have been as infrequent as twice a year. If X.805 framework were used to design and analyze the network, the security engineer would have discovered the need to design and deploy intrusion detection, monitoring and analysis systems. An analysis of the infrastructure and services security layers for the security dimensions of access control, authentication, availability and non-repudiation as illustrated in Figure 3, would have shown the need for deploying missing Intrusion Detection Systems (IDS) and analysis systems in the WiFi networks.

Implementation must avoid depending on the domain knowledge of the IT staff for the correct design and deployment of network security. When a new technology (e.g., WiFi) is introduced in a government network, the CIO should employ a security framework such as X.805. Applying the X.805 framework and verifying that applicable security dimensions are addressed in different security planes and security layers in the project definition, design and maintenance phases, would help to implement end-to-end security requirements.

vides greater capability than traditional Ethernet LANS. With WiFi an individual can move around the premise. If a network needs to be set up in a war zone or a disaster scene, it is much easier to do so with WiFi compared to setting up a regular LAN. It typically takes around three days to setup a LAN for 400 people. With WiFi, it can be done in a couple of hours. Assuming that mobile access points and backhaul are provided, there is no need to worry about cabling, closets and the other parts of a wired network.

However, with WiFi, the signal can be easily captured creating a significant security concern. Another concern is the use of unauthorized or ad hoc networks. Individuals with wireless capable PCs can easily set up these ad hoc networks. These networks would not have the same robust security as the existing wireline networks. The ad hoc networks unintentionally could bridge a classified LAN with the insecure WiFi network. Therefore, WiFi networks need to be designed, implemented and operated carefully; otherwise the entire agency's network could be in jeopardy.

WiFi has various implementations in different agencies. Special publication NIST 800-48 discusses how best to deploy WiFi networks, what the best practices are and how to protect the various access points.

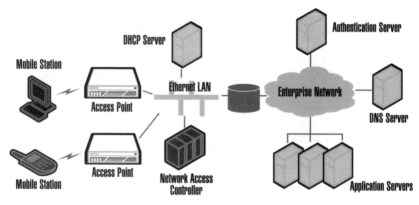

FIGURE 4: A WiFi FUNCTIONAL ARCHITECTURE

With many government agencies moving toward WiFi, it is imperative to be sure that these networks are as secure as possible.

Government organizations vary substantially in their concern about security. The DOD, for example, is an agency with a very high degree of security awareness. DOD officials built a WiFi network in the lab, based on 802.11a, with a goal of providing sufficient capacity for 400 users. They designed a robust network with very strong encryption and proprietary authentication methods to make 802.11a robust and secure. They also circumvented known deficiencies of the 802.11a WiFi network by implementing their own proprietary security methods. To implement proper security design, they leveraged products from multiple vendors.

However, a security framework that can be used to replicate end-to-end security in a cost effective manner, not just by a skillful research lab with large resources, will go a long way toward addressing adverse results. Traditional security frameworks need to evolve so that security design becomes an engineering practice — not a skillful art.

■ ■ ■

S. Rao Vasireddy is a Member of Technical Staff in the Security Technologies Research Center at Bell Laboratories, Lucent Technologies. He has over 19 years of R&D expertise in the areas of data/voice communications services, network security, quality and reliability. Rao's contributions include design and development of IP service architectures, security architecture frameworks and security strategy development for wireless networks. Rao is one of the contributors to Bell Labs Security Model that is now X.805 and ISO 18028-2. He was a reviewer for the ITU-T security manual on telecommunications and information technology. His security contributions have been included in the Department of Homeland Security (DHS) Cyber Security Taskforce and he continues to participate in the government taskforces on security. Rao received his Masters degree in computer sciences from the University of Louisville, KY (U.S.A) and a Masters degree in Electrical Engineering from Regional Engineering College, India. He can be reached at rvasireddy@lucent.com.

[5]

AN INTEGRATED APPROACH TO IDENTITY MANAGEMENT

A bewildering proliferation of passwords, ID cards and PIN numbers is overwhelming users and creating "silos" of inefficiency within information technology systems. An emerging solution to the growing complexity of disparate identity systems is Federated Identity Management (FIM), an approach that makes identity information portable and meaningful across different domains. Here's how FIM can add clarity and efficiency to your Identity Management strategy.

"A CLOTH IS NOT WOVEN FROM A SINGLE THREAD."
— Ancient Chinese proverb

by DORON COHEN AND ROBERT J. WORNER

How can we possibly remember all of our passwords nowadays? Whether organization-to-organization, customer-to-business, or citizen-to-government, more people communicate with each other over computer systems than ever before. Within government organizations, agencies are beginning to offer more electronic services to citizens, streamline interactions with suppliers and exploring new ways to collaborate with other agencies.

Identities play a critical part in any business transaction. The Internet and digital worlds are no different, as the digital identity is not only used to prove who the user is, but also to control and audit the services that the user accesses. Services offered over the Net require management and tracking of identities. The challenge associated with managing and tracking identities is intensified by the growing number of entities — public, private and individual — that each government agency needs to communicate with.

The result is a growing array of digital identities and attendant alphanumeric passwords that make even the clearest minds feel schizophrenic. Users are shouting in frustration: "There must be a better way!"

There is, and it's called Federated Identity Management (FIM). FIM is an approach for sharing and managing identity-related information across organizations. FIM allows an authenticated person to access multiple services in different domains and obtain personalized access without the need to re-authenticate. It eliminates multiple passwords, reduces the inconvenience of the user accessing multiple services from different agencies and reduces the burden of the service provider who maintains those identities.

Simply put, from an end-user perspective, accessing services from multiple agencies requires a single user id, a single password and a single login. Once authenticated to one agency, the end user can seamlessly access services of other agencies without a need to re-authenticate.

This chapter on FIM takes a holistic view of the functions and technologies included within a comprehensive federated identity management infrastructure. It provides an operational analysis on how the various applications of federated identity work. It also provides relevant scenarios that apply to these applications and discusses key technology standards associated with FIM.

In today's heightened security climate, tracking one's digital identities within the enterprise is a demanding procedure. Data threats are growing in frequency and intensity, as identity thieves and hackers become more resourceful and ruthless. At the same time, organizations are under growing pressure to foster information sharing and interact with customers, business partners and public service providers.

Collaboration and interoperability introduce new security risks, calling for appropriate safeguards. Unfortunately, implementing such safeguards involves, in many cases, recording additional identity and access related data in independent identity data "silos", which in turn impede performance and efficiency and undermines efforts for better information sharing.

A plan to collaborate and offer more services — and to do so securely — is no longer a luxury. It is a necessity, requiring new and innovative approaches to identity management.

Consequently, IT managers face a conundrum: How can they offer new services and tighten security measures at the same time without adding new and inefficient layers of complexity? That's where FIM comes into play. It braids many identity strands into a single, interconnected fabric.

The 14th-century English logician and Franciscan friar, William of Ockham, put it best: Pluralitas non est ponenda sine necessitate. Translated from the Latin, this principle, known as "Ockham's Razor," states: "Multiples should not be used if not needed."

To simplify identity management across business domains FIM builds on two pillars — the agreements and trust between the organizations that participate in a federation relationship, as well as a technological foundation that enables a secure interoperable identity exchange.

Establishing trust among parties participating in a federated relationship is a mandatory business prerequisite for a successful implementation of FIM, as the parties trust each other to make valid claims concerning identities that each party manages, as well as to provide secure services to external identities based on that premise. From a technological angle, establishing federation standards is no less critical for FIM, as standards enable interoperability among parties that do not necessarily share the same technology foundation or infrastructure.

FIM extends the reach of Single Sign-On (SSO) beyond the enterprise, accommodating effective management of identities across company boundaries; it reduces the cost of management; it decentralizes the management of the identity information and it allows multiple parties to use the information.

THE RAZOR'S EDGE

Federated Identity Management is an approach for sharing and managing identity-related information across business domains. FIM encompasses technologies, standards and agreements that render identity information portable and relevant throughout multiple domains, enhancing the user's experience considerably.

In many commercial and government organizations, identity and access information is managed in multiple technological and organizational "silos". Each application, infrastructure component or web site may have its own definition of users and access rights to govern user access to its services, resulting in a fragmented identity infrastructure. This approach creates a daunting challenge for both users and IT in managing credentials. Users need to remember and manage all of their passwords for each environment and application. Each application and service provider must endure the cost associated with maintaining and managing all those identities independently. The process of managing the user and accessing right data for each environment separately is inefficient, cumbersome and redundant.

Empirical data gleaned by Larstan Business Reports sheds light on the need for cross domain access. During the third quarter of 2005, Larstan surveyed government executives concerning their systems, security efforts and knowledge of identity management.

FIGURE 1: DO OTHERS OUTSIDE OF YOUR AGENCY HAVE ACCESS TO ANY SHARED SYSTEM RESOURCES ON YOUR NETWORKS?

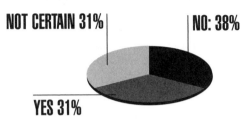

NOT CERTAIN 31%

NO: 38%

YES 31%

Source: Larstan Business Reports

According to survey results, 31% of government respondents currently have a need to access a shared system resource. This significant amount of the respondents demonstrates the need to expose services and resources to external organizations and users. (To download Larstan's security survey in its entirety, go to: http://www.theblackbooks.com.)

The origins of the fragmented identity infrastructure lie in the technological and organizational realities of enterprises and governments.

On one hand, the technology for managing user identity and access has evolved within different computing waves. From mainframes, mid-size systems to personal computing, and from enterprise distributed network infrastructure to the internet and World Wide Web. The history of computing shows us that with the emergence of each technological discipline,

Insider Notes: Federated Identity Management solutions allow each organization within a federated environment to independently solve internal identity management issues using technologies and best practices of their choosing. The organizations become members of a trusted identity network and leverage their internal identity management solutions for cross organization interaction. With FIM, organizations are extending the reach and value of their services, while simultaneously maintaining the privacy of internal users and controlling the cost of user and privileges management.

new identity "silos" were created and employed for user authentication and authorization of user access to resources.

On the other hand, the creation of identity "silos" is not to be blamed on the technology advancement alone. Commercial mergers and acquisitions, organizational restructuring and global consolidation are part of the realities that exacerbate the fragmented identity infrastructure problem by introducing new integration challenges. Within globally distributed environments even an organization that initially practiced consolidated identity management strategy is most likely to find itself with a complex fragmented identity infrastructure over time.

Traditional approaches for addressing the identity fragmentation have focused on the consolidation of systems and integration of identity repositories and processes within the enterprise. However, the traditional approaches of consolidation do not fit all environments because the fragmentation is exaggerated within large user communities. In larger communities, many different users want to operate in a trusted environment and obtain seamless services, whether the service provider is internal or external to their organization.

This is especially true for organizations that are facing privacy, regulatory and legal constraints or operate in an inherent multi-domain environment dictated by their organizational structure. These organizations, such as independent federal agencies, business units of global organizations or partner affiliations, require an approach that extends beyond a central identity management approach.

Federated Identity Management solutions allow each organization within a federated environment to independently solve internal identity management issues using technologies and best practices of their choosing. The organizations become members of a trusted identity network and leverage their internal identity management solutions for cross organization interaction. With FIM, organizations are extending the reach and value of their services, while simultaneously maintaining the privacy of internal users and controlling the cost of user and privileges management.

For additional insight into what's driving these solutions, let's again turn to Larstan's survey. Figure 2 depicts which drivers are perceived to be most important in a federation initiative:

FIGURE 2: WHAT IS THE PRIMARY DRIVER UNDERLYING YOUR FEDERATION INITIATIVES?

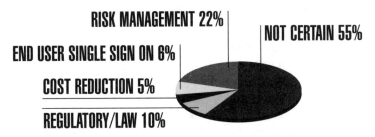

RISK MANAGEMENT 22%

END USER SINGLE SIGN ON 6%

COST REDUCTION 5%

REGULATORY/LAW 10%

NOT CERTAIN 55%

Source: Larstan Business Reports

This survey indicates that managing risk is perceived as a most important driver for undertaking a federated identity initiative among government executives who specified a driver for their federation initiative. It also indicates that a large percentage of survey participants are uncertain how implementing federation will benefit them.

Let's have a look at the benefits and scenarios that are indeed applicable to the government environments.

Insider Notes: In today's heightened security climate, tracking one's digital identities within the enterprise is a demanding procedure. Data threats are growing in frequency and intensity, as identity thieves and hackers become more resourceful and ruthless. At the same time, organizations are under increasing pressure to foster information sharing and interact with customers, business partners and public service providers.

INTERACTIONS THAT BENEFIT FROM FIM

There are four types of government interactions that benefit from federated identity management:

- Government to Citizen (G2C)
- Government to Business (G2B)
- Government to Employee (G2E)
- Government to Government (G2G)

While all of these interactions share certain characteristics, there are different considerations and requirements.

As online business services to consumers become more sophisticated and advanced, citizens demand better services and similar advancement from the public sector, increasing the public pressure on the government to improve service. Therefore, one of the key drivers for implementation of FIM in G2C is improving the service experience for citizens and making government services more accessible.

Privacy concerns around sharing identity information are more pronounced in G2C interactions. As FIM accommodates federated identity stores, a government agency can keep the identity information of a citizen accessing its service private and local, while still providing interoperability and access to other government services and agencies.

As G2B interaction applies to relationships among contractors suppliers and the government agencies it exhibits additional drivers and considerations.

Here, the need for cross-organization interactions is heightened because governments needs to deal with a large number of contractors and suppliers, each with their own identity management intricacies. The government would want to avoid the overhead and costs associated with maintaining these external identities.

In parallel, businesses are looking for ways to improve interaction and business transactions with the government. By implementing FIM and achieving single sign-on and secure transactions, organizations improve their productivity and reduce the costs associated with doing business with government agencies.

In many cases, the government would set up agreements and technology foundations between the authentication and authorization processes of its suppliers from a strong position. The government has the power to define and require its suppliers to adhere to the procedures and standards it establishes, often requiring the supplier to invest in its identity infrastructure to be able to do business with the government.

The ability of the government to enforce standard identity verification, such as strong authentication mechanisms like smartcard, is in contrast to the G2C interactions.

Interactions between government agencies (G2G) or internal to an agency (G2E), demonstrate other drivers that apply Enhancing organizational aspects, such as improving operational efficiency, increasing employee productivity and reducing risk in collaboration between different agencies, takes the lead.

FIGURE 3: WHICH TYPE OF FEDERATION IS OF MOST INTEREST TO YOUR AGENCY?

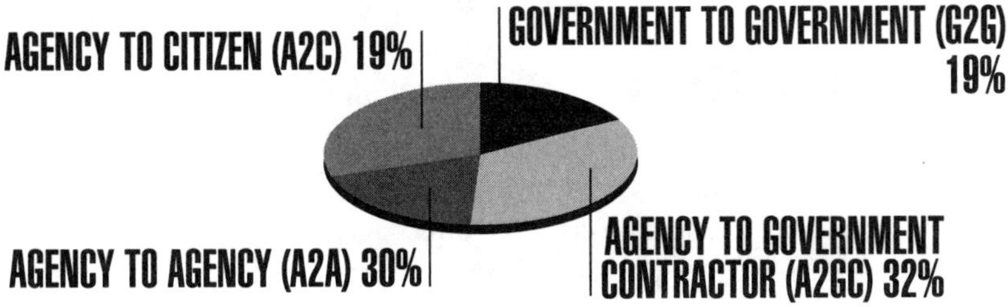

AGENCY TO CITIZEN (A2C) 19%

GOVERNMENT TO GOVERNMENT (G2G) 19%

AGENCY TO AGENCY (A2A) 30%

AGENCY TO GOVERNMENT CONTRACTOR (A2GC) 32%

Source: Larstan Business Reports

The survey demonstrates that the greatest interest in federation are from agency to government contractor and government agency-to-agency. The distribution implies there is a solid interest for the different FIM interactions across the board.

MERGERS AND ACQUISITIONS, GLOBAL CONSOLIDATION AND OTHER BUSINESS REALITIES ARE EXACERBATING THE IDENTITY SILO PROBLEM BY INTRODUCING NEW INTEGRATION CHALLENGES.

There are two basic types of FIM infrastructure models to serve these scenarios:

- The Hub and Spoke Model — a central federation system that supports multiple suppliers. This infrastructure interacts with multiple systems that don't communicate to each other but are suppliers to a common agency. This model is typical for multiple communities that don't know each other, such as Government to suppliers.

HUB AND SPOKE FEDERATION MODEL

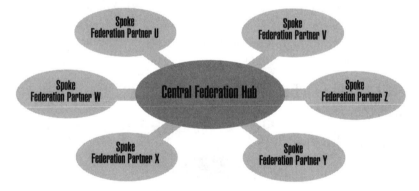

- The Point to Point Model — a direct agency-to-agency infrastructure that requires the identification of individuals across agencies and applications. This option determines the level of access for sharing data as it's for communities that know of each other and must mutually negotiate trust agreements and determine authorization levels. This model is more appropriate to different agencies of the same government.

POINT TO POINT FEDERATION MODEL

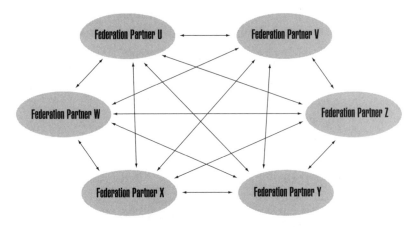

Authentication differs between these models. In the first model, infrastructure authentication is provided by the central federation system. This allows for scalability and expansion of the federation network by only affecting the central system, not the suppliers. The second model, a direct agency-to-agency infrastructure, requires that communicating agencies mutually agree on levels of trust and associated requirements for authentication of the user communities within each agency.

An agency would implement identity federation for different interactions using multiple models in parallel — e.g., service to citizens using a central federation system and, at the same time, participate in a direct agency-to-agency federation infrastructure.

In such cases, it is likely that the federation infrastructure is separated. For example, a citizen would access systems that are different from the ones that suppliers or other agencies would access. Citizens and suppliers would deal with separate applications, data and transactions. Most likely they are different according to the user type, such as a public citizen or an employee. Consequently, even though multiple models may be in action for the same organization, they most likely will apply to different areas of operation within the agency.

FIM IN ACTION — SAMPLE SCENARIOS

There are three key players that participate in identity federation scenarios: the user, the identity provider and the service provider. The identity provider (IdP) authenticates the user and provides the service provider (SP) with the user's details and entitlements. Once the user completes the authentication with the identity provider, the user transparently accesses services in the service provider's domain, as long as the identity provider and service provider have an agreed and secure method of exchanging identity information pertaining to the user.

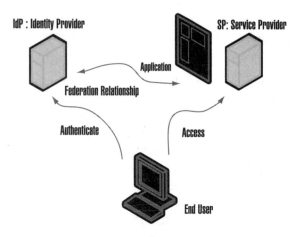

Let's examine how identity federation scenarios accommodate these cases using a fictitious organization — AroundTheWorld.com, a travel agent that provides discounted travel services for government employees. (See below for additional case studies.)

In each of the following scenarios, the Service Provider associates (maps) external users with service access privileges and rights. That mapping may be applied at three levels — Domain, Role and Account mapping.

SCENARIO 1: DOMAIN MAPPING

Domain mapping refers to the most basic scenario, in which one organization provides the same services to all the users of another organization In this scenario, a user accessing the service provider has previously been authenticated by the identity provider, but has no profile or identity definition in the service provider's domain. Nonetheless, due to the trust between the SP and IdP, the service provider accepts the authenticated user, audits her activities and manages the session. Note that the service provider grants privileges to the user based solely on the fact that the identity arrives from the identity provider's domain.

Case in point: AroundTheWorld.com is the service provider, whereas the government agencies are the identity providers. AroundTheWorld.com does not distinguish between different employees of different agencies. All that is required of the travel services company is to know that the person using the service is authenticated by a trusted government agency domain and to audit the activity for further billings and approvals.

Without FIM, each federal agency employee would need to obtain a user name and a password that represents their agency, and use them to authenticate to AroundTheWorld.com. With FIM, the employee agency identification is passed in a secure manner by the agency (IdP) to AroundTheWorld.com (SP), to enable the employee access to the agreed upon services.

Identity Federation enables an improved user experience, by eliminating the need of agency employees to re-authenticate to AroundTheWorld.com. Furthermore, it simplifies administrative costs for both organizations by eliminating the need for AroundTheWorld.com to independently manage and administer users belonging to government agencies.

Insider Notes: One of the emerging demands within federated environments is addressing requirements posed upon IT groups for demonstrating accurate auditing and governance. Without account mapping, an organization allows access to external identities without having a repository or mapping of these identities to real people. It therefore must rely on an external identity store of a partner organization to contain that information.

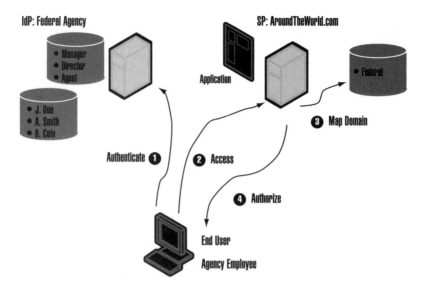

A domain mapping scenario is demonstrated in the above figure. The user first authenticates to the Federal Agency domain based on its user registry, and then accesses the AroundTheWorld.com Travel services domain without the need to re-authenticate. The AroundTheWorld.com travel services domain does not maintain a list of users for the Federal Agency. Instead, the AroundTheWorld.com Travel Services domain relies on the trust relationship it has with the Federal Agency to provide a consistent set of services to all the federated users from the federal agency domain.

SCENARIO 2: ROLE MAPPING

This second scenario refines the concept of domain mapping. Instead of treating all agency employees in the same manner, the authenticated user is mapped to a role and profile that is maintained by the service provider's domain, such as "Administrator" or "Gold Account." The service provider uses this role to determine what services are available to that user. In these cases, the service provider and identity provider must agree beforehand on roles, and the access rights and capabilities that each role, will possess. This introduces a higher level of complexity in setting up and mapping the end user attributes to the services attributes.

In this scenario, AroundTheWorld.com is now required to provide different offers to government employees, based on their title and management role. To fulfill these requirements, AroundTheWorld.com has defined different service levels associated with the title of the employee. When an agency user accesses the travel services, AroundTheWorld.com trusts the agency to assert the user's title, so it is used correctly for travel services.

Without FIM, each federal agency employee would need to obtain a user name and a password according to the level of service they are entitled to, and use it to authenticate to AroundTheWorld.com. With FIM, the employee role is passed in a secure manner by the Agency (IdP) to AroundTheWorld.com (SP), and used to provide the agreed level of service.

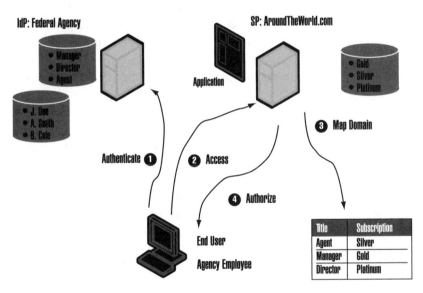

A role mapping scenario is demonstrated in the above figure. As before, the end user first authenticates to the Federal Agency domain and then accesses the AroundTheWorld.com Travel services domain without the need to re-authenticate. The AroundTheWorld.com travel services domain maps the title of the authenticated user (e.g., manager, director, agent) to its own set of service levels (e.g., gold user, silver user, platinum user) to provide the appropriate access privileges. Consequently, when the agency employee accesses the travel services, the access privileges of the user are based upon the title as provided by the federal agency.

SCENARIO 3: ACCOUNT MAPPING

Role mapping is sufficient in many situations; however, some occasions call for a stringent requirement for service access. This need may arise because a business approval or audit is required for each individual accessing the remote service, or because technical application limitations require the establishment of a pre-set account for each user accessing the service. In such cases, the user must have an account at the service provider domain before any service may be accessed.

With account mapping, the service provider maintains a record of each user and is able to govern user access to appropriate services and resources. When an authenticated user accesses one of the services, it needs to provide a unique ID. That unique ID can be either the original identity of the user or, in case privacy considerations prevent that, an opaque identifier that is provided by the underlying federation infrastructure. Then, the service provider inspects the submitted federated user identity, locates a matching local identity for that user and allows the user to access its services without needing to re-authenticate. The local service provider's access management governs access control.

Without FIM, each federal agency employee would need to obtain an individual user name and a password to authenticate to AroundTheWorld.com. With FIM, the employee identity is passed in a secure manner by the Agency (IdP) to AroundTheWorld.com (SP), and used to provide the agreed services the user is subscribed to.

Similar to domain and role mapping, Identity Federation with account mapping provides an improved user experience and service transparency for the user by not requiring them to re-authenticate to the service provider. In addition, account mapping provides the ability to manage individual access control and personalization for federated users. Account mapping, however, provides only limited value in simplifying administration of those identities. The service provider is still required to manage the identities for access control and personalization of services corresponding to the user in the local domain, and synchronize those with the identities managed by the identity provider.

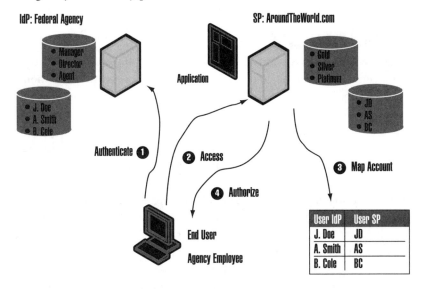

An account mapping scenario is demonstrated in the figure above. Within this scenario, the end user first authenticates to the Federal Agency domain. After authentication, the user accesses the AroundTheWorld.com travel services domain without the need to re-authenticate. The AroundTheWorld.com travel services domain maps the identity of the end user provided by the Federal Agency domain to a corresponding list of local users and their roles within the AroundTheWorld.com travel services domain. Access of the end user is then controlled by the access privileges defined in the travel services domain for that specific identity.

A key challenge with account mapping is the requirement of the service provider to maintain the local identities in a correct state. Each of the digital identities the service provider maintains has to correctly reflect the user identity that is managed in a different domain. Consequently, a synchronization mechanism must be in place to ensure that whenever an identity is added in the identity provider domain, the service provider domain is updated and an account is set up for the user. More importantly from a risk management perspective, it is critical to ensure that when a digital identity in the source domain is disabled, the service provider eliminates the linked identity from its systems. This requirement warrants a cross-organization provisioning and de-provisioning process.

FEDERATED PROVISIONING

Federated User Provisioning ensures that user accounts are in place at the right time to accommodate end user usage of services via the federation relationship. Federated User Provisioning addresses the need to link between disparate user provisioning systems and allows them to communicate in a standard and secure way. As discussed in the account mapping scenario, it is required to facilitate end-to-end provisioning between the identity provider and service provider for account synchronization.

With both role mapping and account mapping, organizations benefit greatly from an automated process and should consider User Provisioning as a key part of their Identity Federation strategy. However, with account mapping, the challenge goes beyond the trust relationship and poses a technology question: Without FIM, approaches used rely on a manual process, email or a periodic feed from the identity provider to the service provider to ensure synchronized identity repositories. However, these approaches are limited to simpler relationships because they are not readily scalable. Organizations looking into FIM look for an approach that easily scales into managing more than a handful of partners and serves a larger trust community.

Insider Notes: Role mapping is sufficient in many situations; however, some occasions call for a stringent requirement for service access. This need may arise because a business approval or audit is required for each individual accessing the remote service, or because of technical application limitations a pre-set account must be established for each user accessing the service. In such cases, the user must have an account at the service provider domain before any service may be accessed.

SCENARIO CONSIDERATIONS

■ **Domain Mapping.** This scenario is the easiest to deploy, because it does not require the service provider to maintain either users or roles from the Identity Provider (IdP). The downside for the Service Provider (SP) revolves around their ability to provide audit. For any transaction or security incident, limited data is available about the individual within the federated access request. While providing SSO capabilities, domain mapping doesn't require cross-domain provisioning, because the SP doesn't need to maintain users or roles.

■ **Role Mapping.** Role mapping is more complex to deploy than domain mapping, because of the need to include role repository and mapping capabilities within the SP's services. However, role correlation is only required between the two organizations, which is easier to maintain than a complete user registry. Role mapping provides improved auditing compared to the domain mapping model, by accommodating an audit trail that identifies role-based information for the user accessing the service.

■ **Account Mapping.** Of the three scenarios presented, this one provides the highest level of granularity. However, it is also more complex to implement. Additional overhead is required on both the IdP and SP sides, to maintain identity maps between the user communities of the two domains. This additional functionality is delivered through self-service registration, with account mapping or through Federated Provisioning. The latter option is more difficult but delivers an automated solution that can be controlled, monitored, measured and improved.

Two approaches stand out for Federated User Provisioning :

❶ On-demand provisioning. With on-demand provisioning, the federation service automatically creates a user identity on the fly in the service provider domain when the user accesses the SP for the first time. The user then may accesses the service transparently without knowing that a new account was just created. The user account would then remain for future use in the service provider's domain until it ages and expires, or is cleaned from the system.

❷ Pre-provisioning of accounts. In this case an out-of-band process occurs by which the user requests access to the service domain. An approval is granted within the use of a workflow process and, eventually, the service provider creates the account for the requested federated user. From that point, the user remotely accesses the service provider and benefits from federated access. This scenario would require a cross-domain workflow and a user provisioning process. There are certain cases when pre-provisioning of accounts is required:

■ When an approval is required from the service provider for the federation of a specific user, such as for license and capacity management. In this case, it is not possible to perform on-demand provisioning. A pre-determined act of provisioning is required using a workflow management tool.

■ When the federated user needs an account in a backend system, like a database, application or operating system, as a technical prerequisite to accessing the service. Here, it's likely that the account must be created and authorized by the administrator of the application before the user can access those services.

FEDERATED AUDITING

One of the emerging demands within federated environments is addressing requirements posed upon IT groups for demonstrating accurate auditing and governance. Without account mapping, an organization allows external users to access offered services without having a mapping of these identities to people. It therefore must rely on an external identity store of a partner organization to contain that information. To satisfy auditing and risk management requirements, organizations are looking for ways to correlate access transactions in their domain with the relevant external identity.

A cross-domain query mechanism for identity data is needed to allow one organization to correlate a transaction with the external identity that is associated with it.

MAPPING SSO, PROVISION AND AUDIT REQUIREMENTS TO FEDERATION SCENARIOS

As we have seen in the last section, there are benefits and cost considerations for each of the scenarios. The following diagram illustrates some of the advantages and disadvantages between the federation end-user scenarios discussed and federation data models. As the table demonstrates, for selection of the right federation model you need to bring into account different considerations:

Scenarios

Requirements	Domain Mapping	Role Mapping	Account Mapping
Audit	○	◑	●
Provisioning	●	◑	○
SSO	●	●	●

○ Difficult to achieve
◑ Limited abilities
● Natural to the environment / easy to achieve

DECIPHERING THE ALPHABET SOUP

In order to realize the described scenarios, multiple technology standards have emerged over the last few years. The growing number of proposed standards for FIM is creating a veritable alphabet soup of confusing technologies. While the emergence of what may be considered to be too many standards threatens the interoperability that FIM is designed to facilitate, this trend also reflects the unsatisfied business needs and opportunities

Insider Notes: Identity Federation with account mapping provides an improved user experience and service transparency for the user by not requiring them to re-authenticate to the service provider. In addition, account mapping provides the ability to manage individual access control and personalization for federated users. Account mapping, however, provides only limited value in simplifying administration of those identities.

that FIM so adroitly addresses. As FIM technology matures, the consolidation of FIM standards is inevitable

The standards being developed are used and implemented to provide interoperability among domains for Single Sign-On (SSO), authorization, provisioning and auditing services. In this area, the prominent standards are Security Assertion Markup Language (SAML); Liberty Alliance; WS-Federation; Shibboleth; and SPML.

■ Security Assertion Markup Language (SAML). This specification defines how to represent security related information about a user in a standard fashion. It also specifies how to use SAML for cross domain Web SSO. The current approved specifications include SAML 1.0, SAML 1.1, and SAML 2.0. SAML is being developed by the Security Services Technical Committee (SSTC), within the Organization for Advancement of Structured Information Standards (OASIS).

Technology convergence in the Federation landscape is evident by the usage of SAML, Liberty Alliance and Shibboleth (see below) as underlying protocols.

■ The Liberty Alliance Project. This group is developing open standards for FIM. It is a consortium of more than 150 companies and organizations that was formed in late 2001. Liberty Alliance released its first specification for FIM in 2002, followed by Phase 2, released in Nov. 2003. Liberty Alliance handles a more comprehensive framework compared with the SAML protocol specification. However, it does leverage SAML for the assertion of identity. Two key specifications by Liberty Alliance include Identity Federation Framework (ID-FF) and Web Services Foundation (ID-WSF).
  ● ID-FF defines a specification entailing protocols for single sign-on, single log-out, federation, name registration and more for FIM as well as cross-domain authentication and session management. The ID-FF was defined to explicitly enable account linking, privacy, and mobile usage. It was contributed back to OASIS SSTC for integration and extension in SAML 2.0.

- ID-WSF defines a framework for identity-based web services that builds on ID-FF. Using ID-FF as a foundation, ID-WSF defines interfaces to identity-based Web services and specifies how to access and manipulate identity-related data in a federated environment.

■ WS-Federation specification is a part of the Web Services Workshop Process. This specification is primarily driven by Microsoft and IBM to advance security and reliability layers in web services. WS-Federation extends WS-Trust to enable federation between two parties and defines two profiles:
  - The WS-Federation Passive Requestor Profile defines browser-based federated Web SSO similar to that defined by SAML and Liberty.
  - The WS-Federation Active Requestor Profile defines how web services clients achieve cross-domain SSO.

■ Shibboleth is a federation standard project run by Internet2/MACE (Middleware Architecture Committee for Education). Organizations collaborating in this initiative include higher education institutions, their partners, content providers and government agencies. As Shibboleth is based on SAML as the core protocol, it is also part of the protocol and technology convergence of FIM.

■ Service Provisioning Markup Language (SPML) defines a framework for exchanging user, resource and service provisioning information. SPML enables interoperable provisioning among disparate systems, by defining an open industry standard for issuing and responding to provisioning-related requests. SPML 1.0 was ratified as an OASIS standard in late 2003. The SPML 2.0 specification is currently in the finalization process and is targeted for ratification in early 2006. SPML is under development by the Provisioning Services Technical Committee (PSTC) within OASIS.

Technology interoperability is a key success factor for the adoption of FIM. However, it is secondary to the legal and trust issues associated with the implementation of federated identities.

One of the challenges that organizations must confront when implementing FIM is identity verification. Identity verification refers to the validation and authentication process that the user performs with the identity provider. It relies on an authentication mechanism, such as a simple password, certificates or a multi-factor authorization. With FIM, a single authentication event allows the end user to access a wide range of services, and more emphasis is required to provide a higher level of assurance that the authenticated user is the real one. Therefore, many federation projects also involve a strong authentication aspect, such as an employee smart card or national identity card. Notably, Homeland Security Presidential Directive 12 (HSPD-12) identifies the Common Identification Standard for federal employees and contractors.

The importance of strong authentication technology to FIM was recently recognized by the Liberty Alliance. In late 2005, Liberty Alliance announced the formation of a Strong Authentication Expert Group (SAEG) chartered with defining a standard industry framework that enables interoperability of multiple authentication mechanisms in Federated environments.

FIM CASE STUDIES
Below are real life examples in which the models and technologies presented above are implemented. Each of these four examples describes a federation type, a specific federation scenario and the technologies and drivers utilized. The situations are real but the specific names of entities are fictionalized.

CASE STUDY 1: A GOVERNMENT FUNDING WEB SITE
Funding.com is part of an eGovernment initiative and allows organizations and individuals to electronically find and apply for competitive grant opportunities from all federal grant-making agencies. The goal of the program is to provide a portal for all applicants of federal grants that enable them to search for, apply to and manage grant opportunities in a secure,

electronic environment. Funding.com is managed by a single government agency and provides services for many federal grant-making agencies.

The federal grants environment is a complex structure that includes a myriad of agencies, organizations and individuals. The individual agencies providing grants function as identity "silos," where each grant-seeking entity must register to obtain an identity, apply for grants and navigate a unique agency process to apply for or receive a grant. This "many-to-many" model is inefficient for both the applying organizations and the federal agencies involved. Funding.com addresses this by centralizing the access and authorization mechanisms and acting as a trusted broker of identity that benefits both the grant applicants and the federal agencies providing the grants (grantors).

The user community for the Funding.com system entails both applicants and grantors. The applicant community is comprised of organizations and individuals seeking to apply for federal grants. Each applicant organization starts by registering with the Central Contractor Registry, which validates applicant information and electronically shares the secure and encrypted data with federal agencies' finance offices. This facilitates paperless payments through Electronic Funds Transfer (EFT). The Central Contractor Registry houses the organizational information, allowing Funding.com to use that information to verify the identity of the individuals accessing the system.

Each applicant organization identifies an eBusiness point of contact as part of the registration process. This individual will become the sole authority of the organization and have the capability of designating or revoking an

Insider Notes: In order to realize the described scenarios, multiple technology standards have emerged over the last few years. The growing number of proposed standards for FIM is creating a veritable alphabet soup of confusing technologies. While the emergence of what may be considered to be too many standards threatens the interoperability that FIM is designed to facilitate, this trend also reflects the unsatisfied business needs and opportunities that FIM so adroitly addresses.

individual's ability to submit grant applications on behalf of an organization through Funding.com. Individuals within the organization who wish to submit applications on behalf of the organization must register with Funding.com. The eBusiness point of contact is informed of each request and accepts or rejects the individual's request for access. Accepted individuals are registered as authorized organization representatives and should have signature authority for submitting grant applications for the organization through Funding.com.

Funding.com uses a credential provider to validate the electronic identity of an individual wishing to submit applications via electronic credentials, such as PIN, passwords and PKI certificates. The individual user applies to the Central Contractor Registry and is provided with a user id and password for the Funding.com site based on acceptance of the registration by the credential provider. Individuals are then able to act independently to submit applications for grants published on the Funding.com site.

The grantor community consists of federal grant-making agencies that produce competitive grant opportunities to the applicant community. These agencies post grants and process applications through data feeds from the Funding.com system. Grantors use the Funding.com site to find qualified organizations for their grant money.

Once an organization is registered with Funding.com and has created the necessary users within the applicable Funding.com roles (an eBusiness point of contact and an authorized organizational representative), the process of searching and applying for grants can begin. Funding.com acts

Insider Notes: With on-demand provisioning, the federation service automatically creates a user identity on the fly in the service provider domain when the user accesses the SP for the first time. The user then may accesses the service transparently without knowing that a new account was just created. The user account would then remain for future use in the service provider's domain until it ages and expires, or is cleaned from the system.

as the identity provider within the system by handling all authentication and authorization services for both the applicant community and the agencies receiving the submitted applications. The agencies do not maintain separate accounts for the authorized organizational representatives. Once the users are authenticated within Funding.com, the authorized functions for the submission of grant applications are made available.

Based on the actual grant submitted, Funding.com routes the application electronically to the posting agency for review and disposition. The individual user is only required to authenticate to the Funding.com system, not to the grant-posting agency itself. The agency trusts the identity of the authorized organization representative provided by Funding.com and uses this identity to complete the actual grant submission data.

Aspect	Demonstrated in the Example
Federated Relationship Type	G2G / G2C
The Actors (IdP/SP)	The government agency is the Identity Provider and the grant-making agencies are the Service Providers
Federation Driver	SSO, End User Experience and Cost Reduction
Federated Identity Scenario	Domain Mapping
Technology Used	SAML
Authentication Technology	User Id and password

The Funding.com system benefits grant applicants by providing a single source to find competitive grant opportunities within the federal government. This simplifies the effort of every grant-seeking organization. Rather than discovering, registering and learning individual agency models for grant applications, organizations now can interact with the standard interface of the Funding.com system and obtain access to all available grant opportunities.

Moreover, Funding.com provides a secure and reliable source for applications to all of the different agencies. Applying organizations are protected from improper application submissions through the standard authentication and authorization model of Funding.com. These protections enable

WITH BOTH ROLE MAPPING AND ACCOUNT MAPPING, ORGANIZATIONS BENEFIT GREATLY FROM AN AUTOMATED PROCESS AND SHOULD CONSIDER USER PROVISIONING AS A KEY PART OF THEIR IDENTITY FEDERATION STRATEGY.

organizations to quickly define and enter their authorized organizational representatives into the centralized Funding.com system, and begin submitting grant applications to all federal grant-making agencies.

Funding.com benefits federal agencies in several ways. By centralizing the identity, authentication and authorization of user communities within Funding.com, all activity pertaining to the downloading, access and submission of individual grant applications can be tracked, controlled and monitored for auditing purposes. Each of the grant-making agencies can leverage this information within the context of agency specific audits. By providing a portal for standardized access for applicants and leveraging the Funding.com infrastructure, individual agency costs are reduced, while best practices are utilized.

CASE STUDY 2: EUROPEAN GOVERNMENT HEALTH (EGH)

EGH is one of the largest health organizations in Europe. It has established numerous Authorities to develop plans for improving health services at the local level and to make sure that local EGH organizations perform well. Within each Authority, EGH is split into various types of Units that take responsibility for running the different EGH services in their respective local area.

As a special project, the Department of Health launched The EGH National Program, the government's biggest technology project to date. In the coming years, the government will spend billions creating an IT infrastructure for a 21st century national health service. The core of the project is a Records Services (RS) application that will provide integrated electronic booking, prescription and patient records on a national basis. Basic patient information and history is centrally created and linked into individual treatment details maintained at the local level.

Local Providers (LPs) are appointed to manage the implementation of national applications in each of five regional "clusters". The five clusters are: City Central; City East; City West; City North; City South. Each cluster's systems operations are outsourced to other companies.

Overall, about one million users will access the RS from various locations. Inherently, the model of independent LPs creates an authentication and SSO challenge for accessing common national resources, such as the RS, since it is unlikely that the multiple LPs would agree and implement the same technologies for their local operations.

When users access the network, they need both local access to local networks and applications within the LP infrastructure, as well as access to national applications, such as RS. Without federation, a separate authentication and login for the local and national systems would be required. This raises the issue of how to reduce the amount of login operations and make sure that the end user gets seamless access to the local and national applications, and achieves an effective end user experience.

The approach to solve this via identity infrastructure is based on a separation between a national common ID and a local ID that is used to access LP services. The common ID is managed via a central national directory, and strong authentication via the use of a smart card to audit and authenticate the users accessing the system. Users access the workstation in the conventional manner: when they authenticate by inserting the smart card, a security token is created with an SAML assertion to indicate the user identity. Now, the system can use the central national directory to map the local identity to the national one, and the national applications can use a security token and SAML assertion to identify the user and their service level. The user is unaware of the diverse infrastructures behind the system and is given single sign-on access to the necessary services.

Aspect	Demonstrated in the Example
Federated Relationship Type	G2B / G2E
The Actors (IdP/SP)	IdP is the LP; the SPs form the RS national backbone
Federation Driver	SSO and End User Experience
Federated Identity Scenario	Account Mapping with Automatic Mapping based on national identifier
Technology Used	SAML
Authentication Technology	Smart Card (certificate based)

A major issue with this model is scalability. As services expand outside of this government's jurisdiction, each LP would need to map the national ID to the additional local identifier.

CASE STUDY 3: VICTIM PROTECTION SYSTEM

The Victim Protection System (VPS) is a cooperative effort among several law enforcement agencies. It is one of 6,500 G2B and G2C applications that are targeted as part of the government's eAuthentication initiative. This initiative provides a blueprint for online identity validation that will enable residents to access government services in a secure, trusted environment with credentials of their choosing. The eAuthentication initiative's goal is to empower industry and individuals to conduct business with government at all levels, using eIdentity credentials provided by trusted institutions.

VPS is a free, computer-based system that provides important information to over 13 million crime victims and their attorneys. Victims receive letters generated through VPS containing information about the events and any defendants pertaining to their case. This information is provided in multiple languages on the Internet and through a toll-free telephone number (Call Center). In many cases with victims, VPS may distribute only one letter. Victims are then directed to the Internet or Call Center for additional information. The government agencies that also participate include:

■ **Investigators**

Depending on the investigating agency, a Victim Specialist will become the point of contact during the investigation stage of the case. Notifications that may be provided by the VPS include the case status, arrest of a suspect, whether the case is declined for prosecution or whether the case is being referred to state or local authorities.

■ **Prosecution**

Once criminal charges are filed, a Victim-Witness Coordinator begins to work with the victim. Notifications that the prosecution may provide via VPS include the filing of charges, scheduling of court proceedings and sentencing.

■ **Incarceration**

If a defendant is incarcerated at a federal prison, victims can receive information through a victim notification program on release-related activities, including community corrections center placement, furlough, parole hearings, escape and death.

Users of the current system receive a letter that contains an identification number and the URL for accessing the Victim Internet System. Using the identification number, the user can log in and request their VPS login id. Under the eAuthentication initiative, the user may be required to appear in person and present identification to a participating electronic credential service provider to create the necessary credential.

During authentication, an unauthenticated user who tries to access the VPS, or any other eAuthentication enabled system, is directed to the eAuthentication gateway. The gateway asks the user for a credential and verifies the user's credentials with an electronic credential provider. The gateway will then share this verification with the VPS application, which will authorize certain access privileges based on the user's identity.

Aspect	Demonstrated in the Example
Federated Relationship Type	G2G / G2C
The Actors (IdP/SP)	The eAuthentication gateway is the IdP; investigators, prosecution and incarceration are the SPs
Federation Driver	End User Privacy and Cost Reduction
Federated Identity Scenario	Domain Mapping
Technology Used	SAML
Authentication Technology	User ID and password

As part of this entire initiative, VPS will be able to leverage the common authentication models of the gateway and streamline processes. The eAuthentication initiative eases the burden on the government in doing business with citizens and businesses, by enabling industry, through the credential service provider model, to provide identity credentials. This takes the government out of the credential issuance/management business, and allows it to leverage authentication work performed by others.

CASE STUDY 4: LAND DOCUMENT EXCHANGE

The Land Document Exchange organization allows participating members to create, sign, notarize, edit, transmit and record documents in a paperless environment. It also handles the fees associated with these G2B transactions. Computer Company Services (CCS) is both a provider of land record systems and solutions for county recorders. It's also a provider of document management and mortgage process solutions for some of the largest global mortgage lenders. This makes CCS uniquely positioned to act as an Identity and Service Provider to the real estate finance industry. CCS plans to offer the Exchange services to its more than 700 county clients in the future. CCS is also creating alliance agreements to enable other counties and companies to participate in the Exchange.

Prior to the Exchange, counties had struggled to automate one of government's most paper-intensive transactions. The recording of land documents leapt forward in the mid-1990s, when imaging technology first turned paper deeds, titles and releases into digital images that could be electronically captured, indexed, stored and retrieved at will. But the documents, so vital to property transactions, still arrive from title and mortgage companies in paper form, signed by the parties involved and witnessed by notaries to ensure the transaction is legal and binding. Even with the advent of electronic forms to automate land document creation and the Web to inexpensively link registries of deeds with lenders and title companies, there has been no manageable way to reliably identify all players involved in the exchange and recording of land documents.

Through the federation services of the Exchange, CCS can manage identities as they create mortgage documents and exchange them with title companies and county deeds registries, without forcing all of the partners in the Exchange to adopt the same technology for authentication and authorization. Users deploy smart cards to access the Exchange. The Exchange is responsible for identifying the users and passing the identity assertion on within the federated circle of trust. A benefit to both lending companies and counties is that as they join the Exchange, they become a part of the circle of trust. This allows them to validate their own users as partners within the Exchange.

Aspect	Demonstrated in the Example
Federated Relationship Type	G2B
The Actors (IdP/SP)	Computer Company Services acts as both the IdP and SP
Federation Driver	Operational Efficiency and Cost Reduction
Federated Identity Scenario	Account Mapping
Technology Used	Liberty Id-FF
Authentication Technology	Smart cards

The lenders also benefit through the ability to use electronic forms to provide faster and more accurate filings. Through a single interface, lenders are able to interact with counties across the nation. With the Exchange, lenders know within hours whether or not documents are accepted. This lowers the overall turnaround time and processing from weeks to days.

The counties benefit from the Exchange through its ability to leverage the authentication and authorization processes. Counties also benefit from the reduction of manual processing that was associated with paper processing.

What formerly took days, or even months, now only requires minutes, or hours, eliminating risks for the title companies and significantly reducing lenders' post closing costs.

FIM: READY FOR PRIME TIME

With the advancement on the FIM technology standards and the adoption of FIM by major Identity Management vendors, FIM is getting ready for prime time.

As secure collaboration demand increases hand-in-hand within the heightened security climate, organizations increasingly require systems that allow individuals to use the same user name, password or other personal identification to sign onto the networks of multiple services in a secure manner.

Organizations must securely share applications, without being forced to adopt the same technologies for identity authentication. FIM gives a single organization the wherewithal to trust another party to manage identities and their access privileges, avoiding the need to manage external identities. Trusting a partner to authenticate its users requires the presence of robust and well-proven security and user-management practices.

Over the past couple of years, Federated Identity Management has matured to the point where technology is no longer the main barrier to widespread adoption. The key challenge organizations implementing FIM are facing concerns the establishment of proper business agreements and trust relationships with their partners.

The government is well suited to overcome this challenge and promote a wide spread adoption of FIM, as it can establish the rules governing interaction between suppliers and the public sector, as well as among government agencies.

In an ever-growing digital universe, FIM proves to be a key enabler of effective information sharing among organizations. To quote Leonardo da Vinci, the quintessential Renaissance man who lived after William of Ockham, but often thought like him: "Simplicity is the ultimate sophistication."

■ ■ ■

Doron Cohen is the CTO for BMC Software's Identity Management Business Unit. He holds a Bachelor of Science in Math and Computer Science from Bar Ilan University in Israel. After spending several years in the Israeli Defense Forces as a system administrator and IT security officer, Doron joined New Dimension Software (later acquired by BMC Software) and has played a leading role in the inception, design and development of the Identity Management product line ever since.

Doron has over 20 years of experience in IT and Security Management, including over 14 years directing development of enterprise-class system and security applications. He has extensive expertise in the development of Identity Management products for distributed cross-platform environments — spanning operating systems, databases and applications. He can be reached at: doron_cohen@bmc.com

Bob Worner is the Director of Solution Line Management, Identity Management Business Unit, for BMC Software. As part of the Solution Line Management team, he is responsible for long-term market analysis and business development of BMC Software's Identity Management Business Unit solutions.

Bob joined BMC Software in 2005 with the acquisition of OpenNetwork Technologies. As co-founder of OpenNetwork Technologies in 1996, he held various positions in the company, from vice president of Product Management, senior v.p. of Product Engineering and president and CEO. Bob has over 20 years of experience in IT and security, ranging from distributed communication network management to heterogeneous security and Identity Management products and solutions. He can be reached at: bob_worner@bmc.com.

[6]

UNLOCKING THE DOORS TO IDENTITY MANAGEMENT

To determine the identity of those seeking access beyond the IT perimeter, governments must contend with the enormous complexity inherent in identifying individuals. To make the right decisions, managers must match identity to dispersed but relevant information – while at the same time, protecting privacy. Here, we discuss the best identity and access management methods, now and into the foreseeable future.

> "SCIENCE IS NOTHING BUT THE FINDING OF ANALOGY, IDENTITY, IN THE MOST REMOTE PARTS."
> — Ralph Waldo Emerson

by DR. ALASTAIR MACWILLSON AND ERIC STANGE

A knock at the door, followed by a response of "Who's there?" This most basic question of identity is older than the tale of Little Red Riding Hood. But with new virtual doors opening online, accompanied by a growing threat from sophisticated

MANAGING I.T. COMPLEXITY IS THE BIGGEST SECURITY CHALLENGE FACING GOVERNMENT I.T. PROFESSIONALS TODAY. REGULATIONS ARE FORCING GOVERNMENTS TO ADOPT A MORE STRUCTURED APPROACH TO INFORMATION SECURITY.

and deadly terrorists, the answer has become more critical, complex and costly. Ruthless cyberwolves lurk everywhere.

These knock-at-the-door encounters occur across federal, state and local governments. At the border, international travellers "knock," and a federal customs and border protection officer must quickly determine whether that traveller is who he or she claims to be, and whether the person's intent is tourism or violence. At government offices at all levels, applicants "knock" to request benefits (payments, licences, privileges), and busy caseworkers must determine whether to grant them. Security guards (human and electronic) scrutinize credentials to determine whether to admit people to secure areas. Millions of times daily, electronic petitioners knock at the door of IT security protections of systems and documents.

Although the nature of each of these environments is quite different, the underlying concepts and capabilities required to succeed are similar. To determine who is knocking at the IT perimeter, governments must meet key security and access management goals, such as:

- Improved Security — better protection from physical, electronic and financial threats
- Improved Service — better and faster provision of benefits (access, privileges, payments, etc.) for legitimate petitioners
- Improved Privacy Protection — stronger safeguards of personal information
- Reduced costs — integrated solutions that cost less than previous and less effective approaches

To accomplish these goals, governments must effectively manage the complexity inherent in identifying individuals, matching the identity to relevant information and making decisions, all while complying with appropriate regulations and judiciously safeguarding privacy.

Identity and Access Management (IAM) is the set of processes, people and technologies that control access to resources in the enterprise. Identity Management establishes who you are and how you can prove it. Access Management establishes and identifies what you can do with your identity. An effective identity and access management solution provides the foundation for an organization to not only comply with regulations, but also manage businesses with flexibility, responsiveness, security and economy.

MANAGING COMPLEXITY

Managing IT complexity is the biggest security challenge facing government IT professionals today. Regulations are forcing governments to adopt a more structured approach to information security and at the same time making departments more cautious in their use of security tools, products and services. Simple tools, such as a photo ID or a password, remain preferred credentials and access methods, despite the increased threat. While governments inform employees of privacy and behavior standards, the security of citizen data is often not as rigorous as it should be.

Identity schemes today are complex and fragmented, either by accident or design, with separate schemes implemented by government functions. The reason for this is that governments drive their security decisions from national priorities, but implement them at the agency/entity level. As the public sector, and the commercial sector for that matter, sifts through the

Insider Notes: Identity Management establishes who you are and how you can prove it. Access Management establishes and identifies what you can do with your identity. An effective identity and access management solution provides the foundation for an organization to not only comply with regulations, but also manage businesses with flexibility, responsiveness, security and economy.

complex area of information security, new technologies and increasing demands are moving at a pace that makes it difficult to keep up.

For example, eGovernment opens up "online 24x7 self-service," without effective identity protection. Moreover, to deliver effective eGovernment services, there is a need for horizontal and vertical government integration, between departments, and among federal, state or local levels, which requires some kind of identity interoperability. There also is a continued push for high performance in governments, with expectations to provide better outcomes for less cost through increased efficiency and effectiveness.

The threat of terrorism and organized crime also drives the need for all government agencies, national, state, and local, to review their own technologies, policies and procedures. At the same time, it has exposed major deficiencies in current practices. Among other forms of crime, identity theft is experiencing exponential growth.

Citizens fundamentally expect their governments to protect them while simultaneously being protected from governments. If governments and individual departments are to fulfill this expectation, they must review existing approaches to identity and access management. They must create a future where the right people have access to the right information and privileges, as conveniently and quickly as possible, while inappropriate access is denied. In this environment, the significance and use of bulky, inconvenient credentials can disappear and be replaced by the person's innate ability to identify him or herself with their biometric identifiers. Once the government (or system) determines conclusively the identity of the individual, rapid information sharing is possible.

To achieve this vision, governments must be able to:
- Establish an identity at first contact that is based on firm truth and credentials, which assure that this person exists and is matched to this identity
- Accurately verify the identity at each encounter to prove that the person is, in fact, the person he claims to be
- Link the identity information to other relevant information, such as program eligibility, security clearance, citizenship, etc.

- Support decision making, by either presenting consolidated information to decision makers (e.g., at the border) or making the decision automatically (e.g., opening the lock)
- Protect the privacy of the individual, by securing it from inappropriate access, as well as facilitating legitimate review and corrections

DEFINING IDENTITY AND ACCESS MANAGEMENT

Data protection and security puts locks on systems. IAM provides the keys for those locks to individuals who need them to enter the right doors. Imagining a business or government using a different key for every single person for every single door, all managed by a different person in a different way, describes the state of identity and access management in today's computing environment.

IAM solutions require a technology implementation. However, this is only a part of the solution. Understanding the transformational nature of the processes and aligning the solution with the people in the organization is critical to the success of an IAM solution. These solutions transform the existing business processes that support the management of identities in the environment. Where possible, manual processes are automated and IT processes are simplified or distributed. Organizational change management and training are also critical components of an IAM solution. In addition, the definition of the organizational structure into a role and permissions model can provide significant value through automation of user access.

The scope and complexity of Identity and Asset Management challenges, and the associated holistic solutions, are vast. Our discussion will therefore focus on the core issues associated with technical components of these

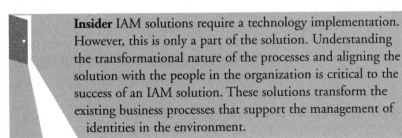

Insider IAM solutions require a technology implementation. However, this is only a part of the solution. Understanding the transformational nature of the processes and aligning the solution with the people in the organization is critical to the success of an IAM solution. These solutions transform the existing business processes that support the management of identities in the environment.

solutions. The key technologies of IAM include Identity Management, Access Control, Provisioning and Identity & Policy Repositories. Integrated together, these technologies provide a platform to support an end-to-end IAM solution.

DELIVERING VALUE TO GOVERNMENT

It is often assumed that the adoption of IAM is largely driven by regulatory pressures on government agencies to sort out the inconsistencies within their internal processes, and within their management of individual identity data. However, for more visionary agencies, the real benefit IAM offers is the ability to interconnect, interoperate and to actually address some of their pressing business requirements. The real driver behind the rising attraction of IAM is the pressure on government to perform several new tasks. These include a plethora of eBorders type work, an avalanche of new demands for inter operative systems and the general desire to allow people access to systems and services to which they never had access before.

At its simplest, it can be argued that government must perform three fundamental roles:
❶ Protect national interests
❷ Serve citizens
❸ Protect costs/equipment (assets)

If we follow this approach, it becomes easy to illustrate how identity and access management policies, processes and technologies can combine to deliver previously unheard of controls for government, as well as improved performance at reduced cost.

The value proposition of IAM in government includes:
■ Increasing security
■ Allowing for innovation and interaction among employees, partners, customers, supply chain managers, etc.
■ Facilitating regulatory compliance
■ Providing a comprehensive audit capability
■ Improving productivity and internal service levels
■ Reducing administrative and development costs

FIGURE 1

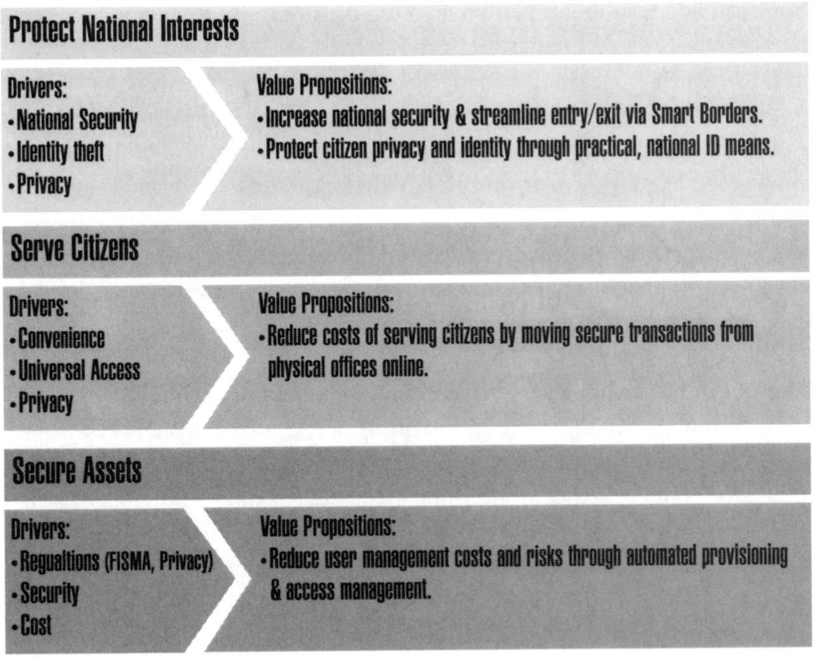

Protect National Interests

Drivers:
- National Security
- Identity theft
- Privacy

Value Propositions:
- Increase national security & streamline entry/exit via Smart Borders.
- Protect citizen privacy and identity through practical, national ID means.

Serve Citizens

Drivers:
- Convenience
- Universal Access
- Privacy

Value Propositions:
- Reduce costs of serving citizens by moving secure transactions from physical offices online.

Secure Assets

Drivers:
- Regualtions (FISMA, Privacy)
- Security
- Cost

Value Propositions:
- Reduce user management costs and risks through automated provisioning & access management.

Figure 1 illustrates the drivers and value propositions for each of these government priorities.

Another way to consider the value of IAM is to assess benefits across three main areas: Business, Function and Security.

BUSINESS VALUE

The business value of IAM centers on:
- ■ More effective management of user access based on business need
- ■ Improved service to users

The big issue for government organizations, in fact for any organization going down the IAM route, is how to maintain control of their users and their users' access to organization resources. That is what IAM is all about. An important business driver is the fact that user administration processes are extremely costly. Features such as call centers and help desk volumes (where users call for password resets because they can't get into an application) can be incredibly expensive in a big organization. Reducing cost center volumes clearly increases user productivity.

A clear benefit of IAM is that it sorts out the problem of being able to audit who does what. It links user identity with their access to different application systems, which simplifies the tracking of exactly what users are doing and ensuring that they are authorized to do it. This is very important from a government perspective and also addresses a second driver, regulatory compliance, which is linked to the ability to provide an audit trail and demonstrate that employees are properly segregated.

Another important business benefit is the potential for dramatic improvement in the quality of service in providing access to systems and resetting passwords. This is linked with improving performance. The issue addressed is the existence of multiple identities for single individuals, a problem that plagues most organizations. Historically, multiple identities have emerged because of the lack of clear identity strategies.

Government is particularly troubled by this dilemma. Agencies might have multiple separate identities for each individual, which costs much more to manage. The intention of IAM is to reduce this identity miasma to one single, ubiquitous identity for each individual that can be used across all systems.

FUNCTIONAL VALUE

Functionally, IAM improves:
- Access administration
- Access ownership
- Access oversight and control

A key functional benefit of IAM is administration, or delegation, of the security administration. For example, when someone joins our company, Accenture, they get recorded onto the personnel system. If IAM is not in place, then somebody has to identify what systems that person needs to access and go through a process of getting that person enrolled on those systems with the right circumstances.

With IAM, people still need to approve the hire, but it is all done as part of a workflow of the provisioning aspect of IAM. An individual joins Accenture; he gets enrolled on the HR system, which triggers emails to that individual's boss or bosses. These managers, in turn, interact and assert that he is a consultant who needs access to, say, 12 systems — do you give approval for that? It's a "click-on-a-box" type of approval, but it is proper approval. Delegation is all about getting the right approvals.

The other benefit of delegation, which is quite important, is that instead of going through a central administrator, these approvals can be pushed out to the business units or business owners that need to get their staff access. Not only are the approvals pushed out, but the administration itself is delegated out to the business units, rather than remaining an IT function. That is an important point, because it means that the process is much more accurate. It needs to go through fewer interpretations, with fewer people involved, reducing the likelihood of errors.

In addition, the people involved are functionally much closer and can give direct authority far quicker than a central administrator. This is a significant change in the way people do things. It pushes the user administration away from the classic IT organizational function and into the business functions. All businesses like that, but especially government, where different departments want to control their own users in a way that is consistent with standards.

Another key functional benefit is the ability to provide and maintain centralized control over system access. A company can centrally manage all policies that govern new hires, security, people changing roles or getting promoted and people retiring or terminating employment. The nice thing

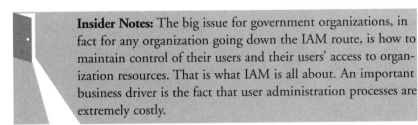

Insider Notes: The big issue for government organizations, in fact for any organization going down the IAM route, is how to maintain control of their users and their users' access to organization resources. That is what IAM is all about. An important business driver is the fact that user administration processes are extremely costly.

IMPROVING SECURITY IS AT THE CORE OF IAM. IF IAM DOESN'T IMPROVE SECURITY, THERE IS NO POINT IN PURSUING IT, REGARDLESS OF THE FUNCTIONAL DRIVERS.

about IAM is that these policies can be implemented electronically, or be represented electronically in the provisioning system. For example, if a policy says that somebody that is leaving the firm must get revoked on all of the systems within 48 hours, the workflow can be set up to make sure that it gets done in 48 hours. Emails and messages are provided to the people that have to authorize it, making them aware of the urgency.

Overall IAM provides fast track access. It gets people to access certain applications in the fastest possible way without any complexity. It also introduces considerable simplicity into their current activities. These clearly are the most attractive benefits for people considering the implementation of IAM.

SECURITY VALUE

The key security value of IAM is achieved through improved:
- Password policies
- Access revocation capability
- Process consistency

Improving security is at the core of IAM. If IAM doesn't improve security, there is no point in pursuing it, regardless of the functional drivers. There are several types of security benefits that would accrue to government. The first is the enforcement of password policies. These policies include minimum password lengths, mix of characters, frequency of change rules (passwords have to be changed every 30 days) and specific characteristics (they have to be randomly generated). Many government departments have encryption systems, which require very strict, stringent passwords. IAM automates this potentially painful process.

Another security benefit is being able to disable user access and privileges instantly, so when somebody leaves the company they can be easily deleted by the fastest possible means. The third security benefit is the ability to manage the identities or the user account throughout its entire life cycle.

IAM also can help overcome the lack of a consistent security framework, especially in government agencies. If an IAM system is installed across multiple agencies, user administration and user processes could be applied consistently in accordance with policy and irrespective of the underlying systems, networks and approaches. It can function as the glue that sits across domains, providing a level of consistency. This is why it's regarded as an integrator between organizations.

It's no surprise that commercial mergers and acquisitions drive a good deal of IAM work. When two banks come together, chances are they use different technologies and systems, and adhere to completely different technology approaches. The only way to glue them together is either by making significant changes to one part or the other, or installing some common processes and systems that allow them to run in a singular manner. Also beneficial is the ability to enforce processes that ensure that people perform functions as specified within stated policies. This encompasses actions like minimum user password links or authorizations to certain systems.

IAM supports important government initiatives. Because one intention of IAM is reduced paperwork, it buttresses the U.S. Government Paper Elimination Act (GPEA). IAM also enables segregation of duties and auditing, supporting the Federal Information Security Management Act (FISMA), which is all about the proper segregation of duties, as well as reporting an audit trail of user activities and controlling their access.

Insider Notes: Governments are challenged by the desire to aggregate knowledge from a variety of sources. This problem entails how to get legitimate access to this information and stop illegitimate access to it. Opening up access to data repositories is one objective, but controlling this access is more important. This leads to government's need to gain more control and visibility over systems.

FACING UNIQUE CHALLENGES

As discussed earlier in this chapter, managing the complexity of security in tandem with competing demands from regulators, citizens and other government departments are the overwhelming challenges facing public sector managers today, as they navigate toward a robust, yet flexible, IAM solution. This important role of protecting and serving is made more difficult by legacy systems, a fragmented approach to public sector management, and the lack of accepted industry standards.

Many of these challenges are unique to government, as illustrated in Figure 2:

FIGURE 2

Government Enterprises Fundamentally Differ from Businesses		
Mission:	**Rules:**	**Scale & Complexity:**
• National Security	• Many laws apply differently to governments than to private enterprises (FISMA, etc.)	• Usually much larger than the enterprises within country
• Citizen Service/Originator of ID		
• Protection of the Citizen	• Citizens fundamentally expect goverments to protect them as well as expect to be protected from governments	• Lack of centralized management of infrastructures
• Enabler of Commerce		
• Fundamentally different types of transactions, examples: Voting, Births, Deaths, Immigration, Defense, Criminal Prosecutions, etc.	• Rules are both legal (laws) as well as cultural, vary significantly from country to country	• Complex high-level security environments

The existence of legacy systems purchased and installed over many years provides a major hurdle for many governments. These systems will take years to transform, replace or upgrade. The inflexibility of these systems is being exposed, as governments face a whole new set of demands to share information between agencies and to more fully understand and utilize data.

Governments have an increasing number of users that require access to its applications and data. This includes organizational partners (within multi-department organizations), customers (the citizenry) as well as contractors and suppliers. The growing variety of these users is a major problem.

However, the biggest change in the last three to five years is that governments have had to open up their systems. Whether a government system is public and open, or high security, there has been an exponential growth in the number of users that need to access that information. It's analogous to algae spreading on a pond. Combine this plethora of users with the growing number of applications that people need to access, both inter- and intra-departmental, and the management challenges become clear. Different classes of users with different security and control requirements exacerbate this complexity of volume.

In addition, governments are challenged by the desire to aggregate knowledge from a variety of sources. This problem entails how to get legitimate access to this information and stop illegitimate access to it. Opening up access to data repositories is one objective, but controlling this access is more important. This leads to government's need to gain more control and visibility over systems.

There also is the citizen's side of this issue. As governments automate customer-facing systems, such as the issuance of driver's licenses, and then correlate this information with passport and other data, they must convince citizens that this information is needed and will be used for the good of the citizenry. How can this be done without inflaming public interest groups that inveigh against Big Brother and Big Government? One way is to demonstrate, that although this personal information is being shared, there are visible and auditable controls that not only expedite the free flow of data, but also protect citizen privacy.

Another major challenge to general IAM implementation is the lack of comprehensive standards. There is now a real urgency to find a common solution. Notably, the U.S. Department for Homeland Security (DHS) wants, and needs, to work with different departments, but they don't nec-

Insider Notes: It is often assumed that the adoption of IAM is largely driven by regulatory pressures on government agencies to sort out the inconsistencies within their internal processes, and within their management of individual identity data. However, for more visionary agencies, the real benefit IAM offers is the ability to interconnect, interoperate and to actually address some of their pressing business requirements.

REAL SUCCESS

Farsighted governments worldwide are viewing IAM as a catalyst for effecting far-reaching and beneficial change in how they secure assets, serve citizens and protect national interests. Below is an example of how IAM has been successfully utilized by a major government in Europe:

■ The Belgian Federal Government

The delivery of services to citizens via efficient and accessible eGovernment systems is a clear imperative for high performing governments, especially in developed countries. In an effort to improve service delivery efficiency and effectiveness, without sacrificing security or public privacy, the federal government of Belgium is implementing broad-based eGovernment services supported by solid user authentication capabilities.

This multi-year project involves national, regional and local government structures. The implementation maintains the fine balance between convenient anytime, anywhere service delivery and the need to foster public confidence and a continued sense of privacy among citizens.

The Belgian federal portal hosts the state-of-the art identity management system, which is linked to personal electronic identity cards or token cards for citizens and civil servants. As the cornerstone of the eGovernment program, the security system enables the federal government to authenticate citizens and civil servants.

Accenture worked closely with the Belgian federal government to build the core eGovernment system, and led the design and implementation of a federated authentication service. It is designed to enable secure single sign-on to applications within and between organizations. The Belgian government implementation consists of a SAML provider supporting the browser/artifact profile hosted at the Belgian federal portal.

The federated authentication service improves security for eGovernment service providers by means of a nationally recognized user authentication standard. In addition, it makes a limited, customizable set of nationally relevant user attributes available to whichever department acts as the service provider. Each service provider can implement customized access rules or personalize the service on the basis of these user attributes.

All levels of government and other third parties can use the federated authentication service, to enable eGovernment services that require strong user authentication. This brings inherent economies of scale, reduces unnecessary duplication and improves the efficiency of state expenditure.

For 2005, over half a million tax returns will be filed electronically by people using their electronic ID or token to prove that they are who they claim to be. The Ministry of Finance did not have to invest in an expensive identity management system to make this possible.

A significant benefit is the substantial cost reduction for service providers that require access to a user authentication capability to offer eGovernment services. The federated authentication service means they do not need their own user registration, management and authentication processes. This benefit includes peripheral cost savings, such as eliminating the need for their own helpdesk support for credential management.

Perhaps most significantly, the federated authentication service of the Belgian federal portal is a great vehicle for providing a seamless, user friendly experience for citizens and civil servants alike when they consume eGovernment services. They can peruse the same authentication credential across a wide range of security domains that have chosen to trust the federated authentication service of the Belgian federal portal. These benefits create a strong incentive for other layers of government and beyond to realize the vision of rich eGovernment services for citizens and civil servants.

essarily have the control or authority over how to do this. If there were standards in place, this would not be a problem.

Therefore, as is often the case, the technology, the thinking and the application of IAM is currently ahead of the standards bodies working to control it. The lack of a consistent security framework, especially in government agencies, is another security challenge. To meet these challenges, an IAM system must be able to align those processes and technology solutions to allow the consolidation and integration of different types of identities within one management structure, and provide individualized security rights based on a person's identity

IAM AS A CATALYST FOR CHANGE

Most organizations appreciate the advantage of IAM. Nonetheless, some argue that its implementation engenders real and profound implications for the unique and difficult challenges that governments face. Although an organization might save $10 to $15 million a year with IAM, it may also incur additional risk while making these changes. IAM is a significant change agent in any organization and it touches almost everything within the enterprise.

Organizations tend to be nervous about large programs that bring change. However, smart government managers are embracing the positive change made possible by IAM, with tangible results. Below is a summary of these case studies.

■ The U.S. Department of Homeland Security

In June 2004, the department selected Accenture to lead an alliance to design and implement the United States Visitor and Immigrant Status Indicator Technology (US-VISIT) program, which will help manage the entries and exits of non-US citizens, verify visitor identities and support visa and immigration compliance.

US-VISIT will help secure America's borders while facilitating trade and travel, as well as ensure the integrity of the immigration process while protecting individuals' privacy — all defined by jointly determined measures. Together, U.S. Department of Homeland Security officials and the Accenture-led team, called the "Smart Border Alliance," are working with stakeholder agencies to design a system that transforms border management through the integration of databases, streamlined procedures, international data-sharing efforts and biometric technologies that support the work of U.S. officials at home and abroad. A signature feature is the planned development of a new type of person-centric, electronic profile that provides real-time information on the status of visitors to the United States.

■ **Belgium.** The federal government of Belgium is implementing broad-based eGovernment services, supported by solid user authentication capabilities, in an effort to improve service delivery efficiency and effectiveness without sacrificing security or public privacy. This multi-year project involves national, regional and local government structures. The implementation maintains the fine balance between convenient anytime/anywhere service delivery and the need to foster public confidence and a continued sense of privacy among citizens.

■ **Ireland.** The Office of the Revenue Commissioners (Revenue) has developed its systems to provide an easily accessible and unified view of their customers. This integrated approach has provided the platform for innovative online tax services, mainly aimed at businesses and the self employed, that allow payment and filing of taxes via the Internet using PKI based security. This has recently been complemented by non-PKI channels, such as SMS, IVR and web forms, for low-risk personal transactions. In the next iteration, Revenue will combine identity and registration security from the Reach agency (which provides the national public service broker) with its own PIN security to offer services to the 2m PAYE employees. Revenue Ireland is one of the few agencies worldwide to combine online service with an integrated back-end solution, thus ensuring its customers a seamless overall service.

■ **Spain.** The Spanish Ministry of Labor and Social Security is making radical changes to its welfare and health services by issuing a new social security smart card for all dependents. The project was rolled out in Andalusia,

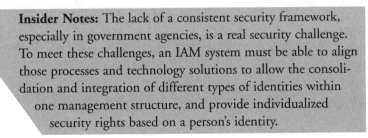

Insider Notes: The lack of a consistent security framework, especially in government agencies, is a real security challenge. To meet these challenges, an IAM system must be able to align those processes and technology solutions to allow the consolidation and integration of different types of identities within one management structure, and provide individualized security rights based on a person's identity.

a large region in southern Spain, and is accessible to 7 million users. Citizens are able to use the card at self-service terminals, or kiosks, around the country, to take care of routine administrative tasks as well as more personal business. As a security measure, the terminals use fingerprint identification technology, allowing citizens to access sensitive information.

LOOKING TO THE FUTURE

The general trend in IAM is towards consolidated identity. Many countries have announced plans for eServices cards or national IDs, or for multipurpose cards by which citizens hold digital certificates. The main reasons given to citizens for the issuance of these identifications are the fight against terrorism, reduction of identity theft and better access to eGovernment services.

There exists a clear need for stronger, automated, interoperable and online identity. Using traditional documents, designed for other purposes, opens too many doors to security flaws. For example, a U.S. Social Security number is an identifier, not a proof of identity (i.e., not a shared secret); a birth certificate is generally used for statistical purposes, not as proof of identity; driver's licenses assert the passing of certain physical, mental and skill tests which suggest the ability to safely operate a vehicle of a given class. None of these were designed to assure identity.

We need:	The solution:
• Stronger identity to cope with globalization and combat organized crime	• Multiple factors, biometrics
• Automated and interoperable identity to cope with globalization and deliver high-performance	• Electronic format for automated and network-based validation (web, phone, email)
• Online identity to support eGovernment and eCommerce	• Should still enable face to face, human validation, as fallback/transition procedure
	• Increased emphasis on enrollment

While biometrics is not the silver bullet for identity management, it is currently the only way to heighten security and improve efficiency in eGovernment, especially in border control/immigration. The optimal practice for security entails three interrelated factors:

❶ something you have (a card)
❷ something you know (PIN/password)
❸ something you are (biometrics)

There is general movement towards electronic ID with multiple biometrics and PKI to automatically identify, authenticate and fill the online identity void for government employees, citizens and the private sector.

Here are examples of notable large-scale pilots and implementations of online identity already underway:

- National ID: U.K., China
- Public service card: Ireland, Denmark
- Multipurpose ID card: Japan, India, South Africa, Belgium, Italy

Culture and historical issues as well as data protection and privacy laws could lead to different implementations of this solution, such as:

- Centralized vs. federated identity infrastructure
- National ID vs. public service card vs. multipurpose ID card
- Compulsory vs. voluntary implementation

SETTING OUT A ROADMAP FOR IAM

Reaching an IAM solution will require various steps. Governments must first conduct a comprehensive analysis of their identity management processes and security needs. To make sure their development is comprehensive and shared, solutions should be assessed relative to the security practices of partner agencies, governments and organizations.

IAM solutions share a common set of capabilities. However, IAM's implementation differs greatly among Internal IAM (Secure Assets), External IAM (Serve Citizens) and National IAM (Protect National Interests). Figure 3 illustrates specific roadmaps for governments to follow in establishing an IAM solution to address these three priorities.

FIGURE 3 IMPLEMENTATION ROADMAPS:

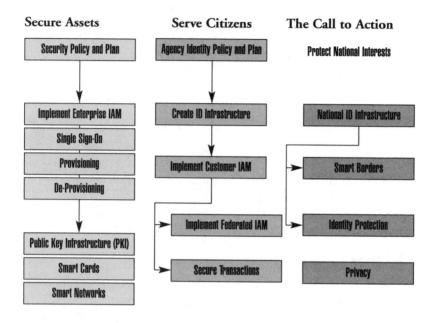

Governments must help educate the public regarding the benefits of effective identity management, assuaging whatever anxieties exist regarding privacy. The public and private sectors also must cooperate and take advantage of their complementary IT capabilities as much as possible, to identify common IAM methods.

This public-private approach will generate synergies by which the sum of the parts is greater than the whole, spawning truly remarkable solutions. An environment of partnership will give birth to many of the tools, processes and (just as importantly) the attitudes that are necessary for successful identity and access management. Make no mistake: to overcome the inevitable institutional biases against new ways of thinking, attitudinal change is vital.

To unlock identity's best and highest uses, IAM must transcend security. Identity not only keeps cyberwolves from the door, it also can deliver innovative, high-performance solutions that efficiently speed the delivery of products and services to trusted individuals.

In this new era of identity management, citizens will see security features not as a burden or a source of fear, but as a means of protecting and leveraging their most important asset — their identity.

■ ■ ■

Dr. Alastair MacWillson is the Partner in charge of Accenture's global Security Services and works with business and government leaders on security, trust, privacy and compliance. He also serves on the leadership team of Accenture's global Technology & Outsourcing Service Line. Prior to joining Accenture, Alastair spent 16 years with the U.K. Foreign Service, conducting international risk analysis. Alastair holds a doctorate in Theoretical Physics, related to research in Applied Cryptography. He can be reached at: alastair.macwillson@accenture.com

Eric Stange has 25 years experience in information technology and management consulting. For the past 14 years he has focused on serving the U.S. Department of Defense in a variety of business areas, with a specific emphasis in the logistics and supply chain area. More recently, Eric has taken on leadership of Accenture's Defense and Homeland Security portfolio, which includes the DoD and Department of Homeland Security. Eric holds a B.S. degree in Commerce. He can be reached at: eric.s.stange@accenture.com.

[7]
THE SIMPLER PATH TO SECURITY

Streamlining the complexity of information technology systems is increasingly viewed among public sector managers as a necessary prerequisite to enhancing cyber security. Conceptually, it all sounds easy enough. In the real world, the challenges and obstacles are daunting. Here, a longtime expert in infrastructure simplification reveals the best methods for achieving this vital task.

"THE MOST DANGEROUS PHRASE IN THE LANGUAGE IS, 'WE'VE ALWAYS DONE IT THIS WAY.' "

— Grace Hopper (1906–1992), Rear Admiral in the U.S. Navy, and a pioneering computer programmer. She developed the first compiler for a computer programming language.

by JIM PORELL

New pressures are compelling federal agencies to simplify their IT systems, enhance processes and cut costs. These pressures include compliance and reporting rules, and budget constraints as well as the need for greater collaboration and interoperability among homeland security entities. For an organization to realize the benefits of infrastructure simplification, it

SHARING DATA ONCE WAS ANATHEMA TO GOVERNMENT AGENCIES, AN INGRAINED ATTITUDE THAT WAS AN OBSTACLE TO SIMPLIFICATION.

must consolidate applications to allow them to reside on a smaller number of servers.

Sharing data once was anathema to government agencies, an ingrained attitude that was an obstacle to simplification. The war on terrorism has changed all that. These days for federal managers, ensuring the efficient sharing of data almost constitutes a condition of continued employment. Indeed, the goal of data sharing now transcends mere agencies and departments and has entered the realm of inter-government cooperation. This major change in philosophy is serving as a catalyst for faster adoption of infrastructure simplification.

Infrastructure simplification is a euphemism for sharing: sharing data, applications and operations. The three keys to simplification are server consolidation, virtualization and automated computing.

SERVER CONSOLIDATION

The objective of server consolidation is to operate a fewer number of physical servers with the same number or less of logical instances or operating system images and similar operational context. This can be accomplished with a like-to-like consolidation, such as integrating a collection of:

- Intel servers into racks or into blade servers
- Sun servers into Sun domains or containers
- UNIX servers into AIX pSeries pHyp partitioning
- Older mainframe s/390 servers into zSeries logical partitions

By operating fewer physical servers, an agency can reduce floor space and begin thinking about simplifying disaster recovery and automating some of its provisioning.

VIRTUALIZATION

Virtualization enables a sharing of some information across logical partitions or across server instances. There are six elements of virtualized sharing:

❶ Data
❷ Applications
❸ Operations
❹ Presentation services
❺ Networks
❻ System images

These elements can be heterogeneous, such as in the case of a large database that meets the needs of several different types of application servers. Or it can be an application-serving portal that manages presentations on one platform but also contacts application servers on other platforms, to provide a consistent input to a variety of different transactions types. From an operational point of view, there may be a centralized security server to provide authentication of digital certificates used by a wide variety of platforms. That security server is centrally managed but remotely authenticated to reduce total system complexity.

Another level of virtualization is in the I/O infrastructure. Frequently, a physically partitioned server will have dedicated memory, processors, disk and tape drives, as well as networks allocated to each individual server instance. By virtually sharing the I/O infrastructure, the disk, storage area networks and I/O connections are shared. This results in a large gigabit Ethernet that shares a virtualized LAN across a collection of guests or partition images. Processors that are no longer dedicated can be shared. They are available to all server images. Hence, the ratio of logical to physical

> **Insider Notes:** The good news is, a wealth of new opportunities is evolving within the industry. New programming and interoperability standards are being generated all the time. Many of these new standards have as goals the reduction of operational complexity and the simplification of decision-making.

DATA SNAPSHOT

Do you extract vital data from your transaction processing systems and maintain seperate duplicate copies within your data warehouse?

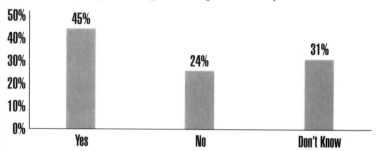

This is good input. The problem this creates is that there are multiple copies of the same information. In many cases, this data may be on different operating environments or within different security administration domains. As a result, actually knowing who has accessed a piece of data, properly or improperly, is more difficult to ascertain when multiple copies of data exist.

Download the complete research study for free at www.theblackbooks.com
Source: 2005 Larstan Business Reports

processors can be reduced to squeeze more capability or capacity out of a virtualized server host.

AUTOMATED COMPUTING

The goal of automated computing is to reduce the number of activities that require human intervention or activity. It allows an agency to have more activities completed automatically, but within described limits and boundaries set by management. Automated computing requires standardized interfaces and alerts, and operational scripts as critical success factors. The ultimate advantage of automated computing is to automate functions within a heterogeneous environment. This could then impact the entire workflow of the agency instead of just an instance or a component within one workflow.

THE EVOLUTION OF DATA STOVEPIPES

Let's examine the essence of the problem. Stovepipes evolved over time as a natural outgrowth of technology adoption. Typically, agencies created applications one at a time. This process originated with mainframes and punch cards, when programming the system was pretty much a workflow unto itself. As a result, there are claims processing engines, human resource applications, POS terminals and ATMs generating reports that are all mainframe centric.

Then other platforms emerged that did things differently. An example of this is large relational databases on OLAP servers. These data warehouses take a read-only copy of the data, mine it and provide insight into its contents. A separate organization was now needed to move that data off the mainframe and put it in this specialized data warehouse server. Other applications evolved that were more presentation oriented or had a better human/computer interface. Later, enterprise applications such as enterprise resource planning (ERP), supply chain management (SCM) and customer relationship management (CRM) emerged. What they all had in common was that they came complete with a dedicated application server and database server. Each of those applications was justified independently within the agency and demonstrated some type of return on investment. As a result, small fiefdoms got created to meet each of these applications' needs.

New applications are continually being installed in most business entities. What occurs during installation is that the business or agency determines the kinds of skills and characteristics the application needs to operate efficiently and then installs it either into an existing domain like a mainframe, Intel platform or RISC platform, or employs a completely separate system, thereby creating another stovepipe.

Insider Notes: While it may be beneficial to sell more servers and replicated data, the reality is that this results in more complex customer systems. This leads to more service calls and a greater expense in diagnosing problems in these complex operational environments.

CONNECTING THE STOVEPIPES

The IT world has now changed. For these stovepipes to exist, data from one must be accessible to the others. To begin this data sharing, a passive connection is established that lets the data from one domain move to another domain. To move this data, multiple copies of the same information must be formed. Some of these copies are read-only but most are read/write. Recently enacted compliance laws — e.g., Sarbanes-Oxley, the Health Insurance Portability and Accountability Act (HIPAA), Gramm-Leach-Bliley, European Union, Basel II — dictate that the privacy of personally identifiable information must be protected. The result is that many companies and agencies may have multiple instances of data as well as multiple policies for managing the privacy of that data.

These organizations are now beginning to understand that there is a cost associated with that redundant policy management. However, since the data is in different server silos and supported by different management teams, privacy protection is not always consistently applied, because the tools used for protection vary across departments. Therefore, when a customer needs to know if their data is being protected, there is no one person or one department whom they can ask.

There is a current trend to share even more data by moving the applications to the data, instead of the data to the applications. This could occur with Java or by co-locating the applications and the data. However, the objective remains to reduce the number of physical instances of the data and to reduce corporate governance and complexity of managing that data.

The question now becomes, "How can an agency host the applications, allow them to be provisioned and enable access to the right data at the right time with the right service levels? And how are these applications managed and presented in a consistent fashion regardless of the domain?" There are technologies that use open standards and virtualization that facilitate this kind of connectivity between stovepipes. The problem centers on organizational issues.

For example, islands of computing currently exist, with each island having its own application servers and data servers and operational needs.

Metaphorically speaking, canals with locks passively connect these islands. There are rules on when and how data can be transferred or copied between each of these organizational units. Now, attempts are being made to share data and the objective becomes to actively connect these islands. Continuing the metaphor, this means removing the locks and widening the rivers and canals into oceans, to create seamless connectivity to this data.

The problem is that every island has its own governor. As soon as more of this infrastructure begins to be shared, the question arises as to who is in charge of this new ocean. Is it one of the prior island governors? There is an organizational component to this problem of getting each "island" to focus on an end-to-end solution and to break down existing barriers. It is no longer a question that one platform is better than another platform, or that one organization manages better than another organization. Instead, it becomes a question of synergy: the sum of the two organizations will add value that can leverage the best of each in conjunction with each other.

One of the problems with this vision is measurement. How is success measured, when there are two different types of servers (for example, a Unix server and a mainframe, or an Intel box and a Unix box) working together to solve a problem that each may have tried to solve before independently? Before, benchmarks were deployed and could indicate which server was superior for which task. But now, when using two servers in conjunction, what should the benchmark be? How is end-success measured? Ideally, success should be measured as the reduction in the number of aggregate physical servers and/or the reduction in elapsed time achieved to get then same workflow. It is also no longer about one workflow, but about multiple workflows related to each other. For example, eCommerce,

Insider Notes: How can existing barriers be broken down and agencies begin to consider sharing data and resources? The simplest way is for them to consider the return on investment (ROI). They must determine how a system-wide ROI will be affected by a reduction in the number of physical disk drives and/or a reduction in security access controls necessary to demonstrate who's had access to particular information.

customer relationship management, supply chain management, and just-in-time manufacturing are all related.

In the government context, a check-the-box mentality often exists. Agencies tend to be more concerned with whether a system is certified at a particular level or what benchmarks have been executed on which part of the system. The fact is that an agency can bring together several certified system parts and still have a "kluge" (i.e., a rudely constructed, needlessly complex ad hoc device) when they are done. There also exists a tendency of looking at how best to leverage each of these parts to the mutual benefit of the organization. Prior to 9/11, the government motto was that every-thing is a stovepipe, everything is compartmentalized and one agency can't see the data from another agency and certainly one country can't see the data from another country. Now it is understood that sharing — especially inter-agency sharing — is an important part of the answer.

Agencies may still want to compartmentalize U.S.-only information from a coalition partner, but the coalition partners are agreeing to share a cer-tain amount of information and they need a computing infrastructure to do that. Real-time access to this information is required — not a copy of the information that could remain live while the user waits for a window to replicate it. Consequently, real-time sharing of data, which in turn means real-time sharing of applications and operations, is a critical success factor for inter-agency and inter-government data sharing.

Provisioning the security to know who is authenticated and who is allowed to share this information and what level of information they are author-ized to get access to are real-time business problems which involve issues such as cross domain database implementations. There are a number of applications in the government for which this is critical.

This problem also occurs in private-to-public sector information sharing. For example, an airline needs to share its manifest with Customs and Border Protection. Banks share information with the IRS to look for money laundering (bills above $10,000) and in many respects there is a high level of sharing there. But now, the government is starting to co-host some of these servers. Consortiums, such as the National Counter

Terrorism Center, are an example of multi-national coalitions sharing data. But these are not much different from what the banks are sharing among themselves today, through Equifax and TRW, to look at credit risk. These types of applications or content sharing have been evident in the commercial space for awhile, and are now being applied more aggressively in the government space and in private to public sector communications.

Simplification definitely affects cost — in a positive manner. With a simplification strategy, the cost question becomes how to share costs across shared systems. Although all costs eventually come down to metrics, the net cost within a simplified system should be less. Let's say, for example, a company has an automobile that gets 35 mpg and a tractor-trailer that gets 15 mpg. If the job is to move a house with the most efficient use of fuel, the company can either dispatch one or two tractor-trailers or 20 to 30 cars. Fuel use varies depending on the work that has to be done. The cars are not meant for that heavy work, so their fuel efficiency is not relevant. The point is that it is not always a cost issue, but more often a performance issue.

In fact, the answers might not be mutually exclusive — trucks vs. cars. Equipment might be moved in the trucks and personnel in the cars. From another viewpoint, the company has a mainframe and several Unix and Intel servers. In a distributed processing environment, this mainframe can be used for real-time batch operations or be tied up behind the smaller systems. With a standard interface, a company can leverage the best of a new application server with the best of the "heritage computing" environment. Performance varies depending on what is used over time, but it also depends on the systems at hand and the work that needs to be done.

SECURITY: JOB ONE

Security is the number one concern for government and commercial entities alike. Everyday there is a new reason why protecting personal informa-

Insider Notes: The practice of leveraging standards is a critical success factor in insuring interoperability among systems, but it's the operational synergy that allows an agency to look at how it can reduce the number of its visible instances.

BY OPERATING FEWER PHYSICAL SERVERS, AN AGENCY CAN REDUCE FLOOR SPACE AND BEGIN THINKING ABOUT SIMPLIFYING DISASTER RECOVERY AND AUTOMATING ITS PROVISIONING.

tion is a critical success factor. This need may diminish as tools become simpler. However, all of these tools must work in a heterogeneous environment. It is no good to solve security on only one platform if that platform interoperates with another one. It is up to the business to provide the glue that secures a heterogeneous system; otherwise, the security problems will last for years.

That is why leveraging open standards is a critical success factor to facilitate inter-domain authentication and access control. Even as far back as the Middle Ages, castles with moats had drawbridges to facilitate a movement of materials and subscribed to certain safeguards for managing that gate. The same is true in a mixed-system information technology environment. "Fences" can be built around each administrative domain, but then that organization will require interoperability with another organization and an agreement must be established to facilitate that interoperation.

The mainframe model is to share all data across all homogeneous mainframe server images. Other platforms like Intel or RISC-based systems, as well as the mainframe, can use both networked attached storage as well as storage area networks that leverage a common format and protocol with which they access the data. The objective is to have common access to data.

There is more and more being done now to reduce the size of the protocol and provide more direct access to data sharing instead of network access to sharing. The reason for direct sharing of data is that network access to data sharing doesn't establish the necessary level of confidentiality nor efficiently manage bandwidth being shared between applications and data over the intranet and Internet environments. Direct access to data will reduce some of that separate storage area network from the intranet environment that will help further compartmentalize access to the data. Access to the data will still have to be secured via authentication, but this physical separation will provide another level of protection.

TECHNOLOGY PIVOT POINTS FOR SIMPLIFICATION

Let's discuss storage topologies and ways to reduce risk by storing only one instance of data. The primary means of transferring data today is with FTP (File Transfer Protocol). This program can transfer data securely within a virtual private network or with SSL or TLS security. However, sharing data is a different matter. There is only one instance of data and it must be shared.

There are several technologies that can facilitate the sharing of data across heterogeneous systems. One is a network attached storage technology commonly called the network file system (NFS), the common Internet file system embodied by SAMBA and open source technologies. With NFS, clients from multiple computers can share the same data whether it's text, application binaries or a program's source code.

A second technology that has recently evolved is the storage area network system (SAN). SAN's uses either SCSI or a storage network to share data instead of going over an Intranet or Internet. This is perceived as direct access to these storage disks. In a SAN environment, the data is physically moving. However, instead of moving over the Internet, it's moving over the storage network, which by definition eliminates some security risks. Different physical security for the storage network will reduce some risk. Otherwise, it's the same inherent formats and security between the two components.

In the database arena, the ODBC and JDBC protocols can be leveraged to make distributed connections to a database. This method has existed for

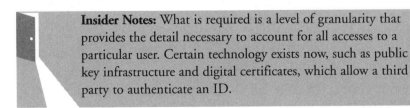

Insider Notes: What is required is a level of granularity that provides the detail necessary to account for all accesses to a particular user. Certain technology exists now, such as public key infrastructure and digital certificates, which allow a third party to authenticate an ID.

DATA SNAPSHOT

How often are your web service applications developed separately from your transaction processing applications?

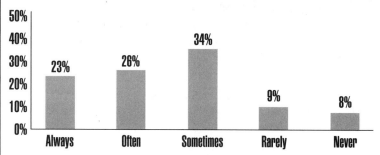

This can be another hidden cost of computing. With close to 50% responding that the programs are independently built, there can be additional costs in burning new MIPs in the transaction processing environment. There are also additional complexities in authentication and audit work flows when they are developed and/or operated and administered independently.

Download the complete research study for free at www.theblackbooks.com
Source: 2005 Larstan Business Reports

years; the difference now is that an agency might want to direct a data request to the original source of data, such as a transaction processing system, instead of a data image made from a copy or extract of the transaction processing system.

The main security benefit of these technologies is that there is only one instance of data, or a shared instance of data. This enables a more granular analysis of who's had access to this data. This simplifies governance issues and the management of personally identifiable information. Each time the data is copied, the policies controlling it are also replicated. If the data moves from one server architecture to another one, the tools for managing compliance and doing audits are different in many cases. A new level of effort is now required to correlate these policies on behalf of users. For example, did this IRS ID or Social Security number get misused in some way because it wasn't protected properly, or because a different policy was used by one department or agency versus another one?

NETWORKING TOPOLOGIES

Two networking architectures define the current environment. The older mainframes, which are predominantly IBM, utilize SNA (system network architecture) and the other networking environments are based on TCP/IP. There also exist differences between TCP/IP and the Internet protocols that primarily use token ring versus Ethernet as a physical topology.

Some agencies may have adopted token ring or ATM technology, which is more expensive to host, and are now trying to install more state-of-the-art commodity-based hardware and network protocols. However, some of the resident applications actually had to understand the networking topology. Fortunately, a rework of those applications is not necessary. There are emulation techniques available to share the physical network on a zSeries with the mainframe, because the SNA hardware embodied by hardware such as the 37/45 "communication" controller can now be emulated in a Linux for zSeries partition or guest on the same server box.

The critical point is that the mainframe application will still speak in SNA architecture, but this will be translated in this Linux instance into an Internet protocol, which means less expensive computing devices can be used. This, in turn, reduces the footprint for the SNA hardware. Re-hosting within an existing application reduces capital, environmental and maintenance costs. Again, these cost savings are achieved system wide, end-to-end, not just one stovepipe at a time.

EMERGING SECURITY MECHANISMS

Security mechanisms are one of the most valuable areas to consider in terms of simplifying regulation and compliance. Each variety of server operating system (Windows, Linux, Unix, mainframe z/OS) might have its

Insider Notes: The mainframe model is to share all data across all homogeneous mainframe server images. Other platforms like Intel or RISC-based systems, as well as the mainframe, can use both networked attached storage as well as storage area networks that leverage a common format and protocol with which they access the data. The objective is to have common access to data.

own specific local security server. As a result, when work comes in to those servers, the users' IDs must be authenticated, and then, using that authentication, access to resources on that server image (whether it's application or database oriented) must go against that local security server. The more different platforms being deployed, the more security flows that get executed end-to-end. Consequently, there is a wealth of companies who sell "single sign-on" solutions that really aren't single sign-on. They are multiple sign-ons, but incorporate meta-directories that translate one user ID to another one.

The problem emerges with audit and compliance tools: how is meta-mapping correlated from one system to another? Or is the system using many-to-one mapping? All of these end-to-end consumers are mapped to a global server ID. It is apparent that the server accessed a certain piece of the database. What is unclear is whose context, or what individual user or client request that came into that server, actually got access to the data.

What is required is a level of granularity that provides the detail necessary to account for all accesses to a particular user. Certain technology exists now, such as public key infrastructure and digital certificates, which allow a third party to authenticate an ID. Then that user ID can be authenticated and mapped locally to a security context for application access control.

There isn't any state-of-the-art distributed access control mechanism that works for all resources. However, there are some emerging technologies such as Tivoli Access Manager, or ezSignon from Vanguard Integrity Professionals, that will provide some common distributed access management, particularly with application types such as Web services. The ultimate objective, however, is to leverage these technologies in order to share authentication and access control. This will enable end-to-end auditing of all the resources from initial sign-on to a PC, to a Web portal, to a Web service, to database access, and then to a business process integration workflow. The same ID context must be mapped throughout, so information becomes available on who has seen critical system information and personally identifiable objects, and who might have modified or updated a particular resource.

APPLICATION SHARING: A STARRING ROLE

Application sharing plays a very big role in infrastructure simplification. There are several areas in which systems can be simplified by sharing applications. To begin, there still exists a wealth of legacy, or heritage applications, on which the foundation of an agency or business has been built. But these systems still may have a front end that's oriented toward a punch card or green screen command line. That's pretty boring in this graphically enabled Palm Pilot and BlackBerry personal computing device era (or pervasive computing device era). That means the agency would like to bridge the two, and leverage the new human factors of these pervasive computing devices (kiosks, Web browsers, PDAs, etc.) while maintaining the business logic resident in the traditional or heritage computing applications.

This can be done either by rewriting the traditional applications, to take advantage of the new architectures, or by modifying the middle-ware to support both the old green screen and the new service-oriented architectures. Modifying the front end can yield a multi-modal transformation and yield a consistent back end application environment to meet the organization's needs.

To accomplish this type of sharing, technologies such as Web portals that are close to the front end of the pervasive computing devices need to be used to do the transformation of the information. In tandem, the application servers that are close to the traditional transaction manager systems can often provide a seamless merger of multiple heritage transaction systems into one new service, hence simplifying operations. Then, Web services can be used at both the presentation side and at the application or database serving side to create a new workflow and really modernize the system while minimizing the conversion or reengineering effort. In some

Insider Notes: Security is the number one concern for government and commercial entities alike. Everyday there is a new reason why protecting personal information is a critical success factor. This need may diminish as tools become simpler. However, all of these tools must work in a heterogeneous environment.

DATA SNAPSHOT

Does your organization apply a separate and unique security authentication for user access for each application server?

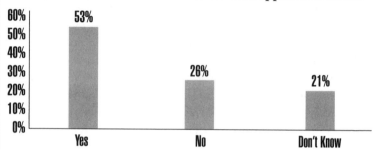

The concern here is that often several applications might participate in a business workflow. With separate administration domains, audit and compliance become more difficult. Risk occurs when data is correlated across these administration boundaries.

Download the complete research study for free at www.theblackbooks.com
Source: 2005 Larstan Business Reports

respects, this would leverage the best of all worlds, the back end serving, the front end serving, as well as the new presentation devices.

This becomes a natural extension into presentation sharing. This is the second area of application sharing which is determining how much knowledge is required on the individual desktop to host this new workflow presentation. The issue is whether a special code or a special browser or reader is required on the user desktop and whether the user will have to manage all of the plug-ins. Or, perhaps the desktop can be virtualized.

A second issue is whether some of that application-serving and presentation-serving can be hosted at the back end, in a blade center or in a rack of computers, allowing users to work with thin client and employing applications like Citrix Metaframe or a Linux hypervisor to leverage a thin client desktop. In this manner, all of the correct readers would be resident on that presentation server, and the amount of overhead and management at some of the office desktops in various agencies would be reduced. Thin clients will not be used by power-users, but they can be used in an office environment (spreadsheets, presentations, word processing, Web browsing and such). This is another method to simplify infrastructure and reduce end-to-end costs.

TESTING THE OPERATIONAL METTLE

Virtualization has been discussed in this chapter, as it is applied to data, applications, presentations and networks. Virtualization also applies to operations. When stovepipes are being managed independently, each one has its own storage management, its own disaster recovery plan for both high availability and continuous availability, and its own content. Yet, in reality, one server is just participating in a workflow with other servers. Therefore, it is critical that operational planning for business resilience, for security and for continuous availability be shared across the entire heterogeneous computing mix.

The practice of leveraging standards is a critical success factor in insuring interoperability among systems, but it's the operational synergy that allows an agency to look at how it can reduce the number of its visible instances. For example, when an application can be brought to the data or the application can be pointed to the data on one platform automatically, across stovepipes, several instances of complexity are addressed. First, it eliminates the need of having two separate organizations agree on how the data will be moved. Second, there is now no need to run new applications to synchronize the data exchanged between these two replicated platforms. As a result, operational complexity is reduced, less MIPs are consumed and less space capital is required.

Insider Notes: Prior to 9/11, the government motto was that everything is a stovepipe, everything is compartmentalized and one agency can't see the data from another agency and certainly one country can't see the data from another country. Now it is understood that sharing – especially inter-agency sharing – is an important part of the answer.

WE CAN ALSO GLEAN VALUABLE LESSONS FROM WHAT DOESN'T WORK. THE MOST IMPORTANT PITFALL FOR ALL ORGANIZATIONS IS A LACK OF KNOWLEDGE OF WHAT IS AND IS NOT INSTALLED. IT COULD BE CALLED "STEALTH ARCHITECTURE."

Organizational boundaries affect simplification efforts. There is a wealth of technology available to help facilitate a level of infrastructure simplification, but these efforts are often stymied when organizational boundaries need to be crossed. When this happens, issues arise, such as who the decision-makers are and how they make those decisions. In addition, there is the issue of how results are quantified. Currently, it is difficult to quantify results in a shared environment. Typical benchmarks are done one server, one application or one database at a time. But simplification requires operational aggregation and nobody in the industry has focused on how to blend different computing types together to break down these barriers to measurement. However, there are a number of efforts underway to look at this issue.

When considering the impact of government fiefdoms on simplification, the most prominent example is the U.S. Department of Homeland Security. This department is really an amalgamation of 22 agencies brought together under one giant umbrella. Each agency had its own competing infrastructure and it was probably, at one time or another, consumed within a different agency. For example, Customs and Border Protection used to be under the Treasury Department, so it had some opportunity to share operations with Treasury. Therefore, it is important to look at how to preserve those legacy agency-to-agency connections as well as to accommodate the new emerging agency connections.

This phenomenon also occurs in public/private sector interaction. Again using Customs and Border Protection as an example, this agency looks to the airlines, the ground transportation industry and shipping manifests to complete all kinds of analysis prior to departure or upon entry into the country, for immigration and customs duty payment purposes. The process of sharing data already exists among numerous agencies and among agencies and private entities. These must be leveraged in any simplification effort.

How can existing barriers be broken down and agencies begin to consider sharing data and resources? The simplest way is for them to consider the return on investment (ROI). They must determine how a system-wide ROI will be affected by a reduction in the number of physical disk drives and/or a reduction in security access controls necessary to demonstrate who's had access to particular information. It is intuitively obvious that with fewer moving parts, the system is a less complex operational environment, and more easily managed.

However, the real question becomes who's in charge of this reenergized or reinvigorated organization — this new fiefdom? That is more difficult. At which levels within the civil service do these executives operate and how will they achieve their next level of success? Is it through operational management? By defining IT managers' roles through successful operational management, agencies might actually reduce complexity, by ending the prevalent "rip-and-replace, start-from-scratch" mentality. This mentality exists within the 6-10 year reengineering process and, in parallel, within the management of the existing network environment.

Efforts to reduce complexity should have many benefits including: speeding the deployment of new technologies; addressing the private to public acceptance of a new infrastructure; and simplifying how one nation shares information with other nations within coalitions, such as "Operation: Iraqi Freedom" and in counter-terrorism efforts.

Insider Notes: The IT world has now changed. For stovepipes to exist, data from one must be accessible to the others. To begin this data sharing, a passive connection is established that lets the data from one domain move to another domain. To move this data, multiple copies of the same information must be formed.

ATTEMPTS ARE BEING MADE TO ACTIVELY CONNECT ISLANDS OF DATA. THIS MEANS REMOVING THE LOCKS AND WIDENING THE RIVERS AND CANALS INTO OCEANS, TO CREATE SEAMLESS CONNECTIVITY.

THE ENDURING BATTLE AGAINST COMPLEXITY

Within IBM, there are numerous efforts, mostly within the "on-demand" operating environment, where heterogeneous distributed computing and multi-vendor environments are considered to help customers simplify. While it may be beneficial to sell more servers and more and more replicated data, the reality is that this results in more complex customer systems. This leads to more service calls and a greater expense in diagnosing problems in these complex operational environments. In other words, attracting customers to simplified infrastructures also benefits IBM.

Since most environments are multi-vendor, it is important to develop and follow standards. There are standards for distributed databases. There's a suite of the J2EE operational standards, and the IETF manages the evolving Internet protocols. As important are compliance tests to insure that a particular piece of code meets the existing standards. IBM conducts "bake-offs" for interoperability, for security, database sharing and virtual private networks to ensure that they will inter-operate and provide secure communications.

New consortiums also are being created and new standards evolving to facilitate the next generation of Web services distributed management; WSDM is an example of these new standards. Alliances also are being forged to facilitate security sharing. For example, Identrust compliance is used for digital certificate processing for inter-bank transfers. This consortium is made up of a number of the large banks and some of the digital certificate suppliers.

Therefore, the key to influencing, maintaining, adopting and delivering, upon standard or "open" technologies, is an open environment that can facilitate this heterogeneous operation and sharing of resources. IBM, along with other vendors, is actively working in this space to meet the spirit of on-demand operating environments and reduce customers' complexity.

OBSTACLES TO SIMPLIFICATION

The conceptual path to simplification is clear, but in reality it's strewn with many obstacles.

Technological. Ironically, there exists such a wealth of technologies and opportunities that allow an agency to simplify their infrastructure, that no single agency understands all the possible methods available to it. Since most organizations are still stovepipes, one agency might know its part works, but may not necessarily be aware of other capabilities on other platforms that might also be necessary or applicable to its mission. Or worse, they might not know what other platforms are in use at other organizations.

The stovepipe deployment structure results in each application server or each organization having its own server infrastructure without concern as to what other agencies have. Consequently, there exists a technical obstacle in terms of knowing what capabilities are available.

Organizational. One of the difficulties of getting two government agencies to collaborate is the need to assign a project manager, a requirement for all government projects. When two separate organizations, and their attending political fiefdoms, try to collaborate, there could be difficulty in terms of providing one team the power to determine the direction for another team. Or, one team might view this reorganization as a means to obtain additional power. This can inhibit collaboration because the two agencies are not necessarily working together toward a common goal but

Insider Notes: The goal of automated computing is to reduce the number of activities that require human intervention or activity. It allows an agency to have more activities completed automatically, but within described limits and boundaries set by management. Automated computing requires standardized interfaces and alerts, and operational scripts as critical success factors.

SIMPLIFICATION IN THE REAL WORLD

Case studies provide powerful testimony to the assertions made in this chapter. This section examines generalized — but real-world — examples of the methods and theories you've been reading.

Let's spotlight an organization that collects information or provides commerce, such as an Internal Revenue Service or a Customs and Border Protection agency. These agencies are essentially transactional environments. They receive an e-file or a border crossing, and information is stored. Later, that data could be processed for an audit or for operational risk assessments.

In this manner, another system might capture that data and leverage it. Along the way, there could be included a tremendous amount of personally identifiable information, especially when considering something like taxes. Making copies of that data to process independently increases the operational risk of disclosure. Any time that there are more copies of data, there are more opportunities for risk and more opportunities for management.

The objectives for these agencies to simplify would be:
- To reduce data moves and bring the applications back to the data
- To figure out ways to synergistically share that information
- To provide access methods or a service oriented architecture that defines a standard access method for that data

The result would be reducing operational risk, compliance with regulations and protection of the data. Therefore, leveraging file sharing technologies and sharing database infrastructures are vehicles for simplifying infrastructure and simplifying data management.

Another example is the use of a Web portal. An agency or a department might create a Web presence. If its sub-agencies each create an independent Web presence, then, in essence, they are creating an independent personality with redundant infrastructure. By considering common Web servers and common security for those Web servers they could begin to leverage a portal to personalize the experience for whomever the end-user is; whether it is an analyst within an agency, a department member or Congress. Different levels of input and knowledge would share data, depending on whether it is a business to government, or consumer/private citizen to government exchange. A common front end and a common information disbursement or deployment can be used to simplify how or who gets access and to create a reporting structure for the infrastructure.

Some large government departments might have multiple sub-agencies and they can get into tremendous complexity if each one independently recreates similar capabilities, like a portal, security authentication or file serving structures. It would also result in redundancy in backup/archive, migration/recall, disaster recovery and continuous availability solutions. Sharing some of that data and application or presentation-serving infra-structure can assist in reducing the overall cost and redundancy across organizational boundaries.

LEARNING FROM COMMON MISTAKES

We can also glean valuable lessons from what doesn't work. The most important pitfall for all organizations is a lack of knowledge of what is and is not installed. It could be called "stealth architecture." There are many new features and functions that have been added to the base oper-ating systems, at no additional charge, that are installed but not being deployed. The reason is that, since there is no charge for this added capability, there is no incentive for anyone to sell it or introduce it as a new capability. If a customer keeps abreast of all the latest IBM (as well as other vendors') announcements, reviews their Website and keeps up with company news feeds, they might know of these new technologies and capabilities. If not, those new system capabilities can be missed.

Customers that see the new technologies, without a description of how they work, might not deploy it. A good example is z/OS. This operating system now ships with the network file system (NFS) server, both client and server. A mainframe operator would look at that and say that it's interesting, but what can it be used for? However, if this customer does application development on an Intel platform, which is deployed on a mainframe, and they leverage Websphere that needs some Java code, they will need copies of Java .jar files on each desktop and the mainframe. Or, they can put it on a file server that is shared. Since it is the same code, it works in both places and the customer will have one instance of data and one backup recovery plan.

Another z/OS example is that it now ships with public key infrastructure and digital certificate management for business. The customer may not have any applications currently on the mainframe that will take advantage of this capability, but is using digital authentication on another platform. Therefore, that customer is paying for that other vendor's certificate authority on a certificate basis and paying for those other servers that are typically standalone, whereas they already have paid for the mainframe with this certificate authority.

Moreover, as the customer leverages the public key infrastructure on the other platforms, what are the points of control? How many audit points will they have? By putting it into the mainframe where audit is already established as an important business practice for protecting transaction processing and databases, the customer has the ability to leverage a trust authority in a common place to meet the needs of all the Intel and other servers that are in the enterprise. Again, the technology is there, but the customer doesn't know how to use it because typically that decision point was in a different fiefdom.

Conversely, in a blade environment, new blade centers are evolving which create hosted client functionality or enable thin clients. A customer may think that they do not need thin clients. However, if they do not manage changes on their PCs nor update PC technology because it is too tedious to touch every PC, using thin clients can reduce the complexity of these changes. The thin client will have a regular terminal with a keyboard, mouse and screen but the actual logic is stored on the centralized server. Individuals can still personalize their desktops but change is now centralized. This confers reduced system complexity. The customer can speed up the deployment of new technology, new applications and new infrastructure. That's another way to "virtualize" the presentation capability.

instead are working toward a political goal. One way to address this is to find somebody with no vested interest in the results to be the project manager. Then the business problem may actually be tackled, versus grappling with an organizational or philosophical problem.

Within the government the organizational problems and pitfalls can be more severe, because personal issues such as political appointments versus civil service appointments or differences in graded positions can also negatively impact a collaborative effort. In addition to the politics that may occur in the organization or an agency, congressional oversight and the U.S. Office of Management and Budget (OMB) also have a distinct say and influence over a particular deployment.

There also exist agency specific issues: for example, within the intelligence community, there exists DCID 6-3 (DCID is Department of Central Intelligence Directive), a directive on how certain departments must certify the operations of their specific programs. Overlying all of these inter-agency issues are the standards or approved government technology managed by NIST or NIAP. This includes technology approved in the federal information processing standards (FIPS) and common operating environment (COE) of the Department of Defense. These standards can strongly influence if and how a particular technology or component can be deployed.

The good news is, a wealth of new opportunities is evolving within the industry. New programming and interoperability standards are being generated all the time. Many of these new standards have as goals the reduction of operational complexity and the simplification of decision-making. However, it is still up to the individual agency to determine when and if they will leverage those technologies to provide a less expensive and a more simplified infrastructure for their agency.

INTERAGENCY SIMPLIFICATION, STEP BY STEP

There is a tremendous opportunity to simplify within agencies. Some of these agencies are huge and have many sub-agencies or departments. Starting there, within one large agency there will be a greater chance to establish a model for simplification. Diving right into inter-agency simplification there will be no proof-point that it will work. By establishing a

DATA SNAPSHOT

What is the lowest, most granular level within your organization by which compliance with regulations is administered?

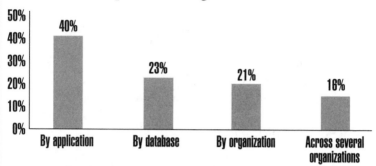

Again, this can raise the complexity of soliciting and correlating audit records across a workflow for an individual's access. While correlating this info after the fact may aid in detecting a potential data leakage exposure, it can add complexity to actually preventing a real-time data leak. Detection mechanisms, after the fact, are often too late to prevent harm or misuse.

Download the complete research study for free at www.theblackbooks.com
Source: 2005 Larstan Business Reports

proof-point within a single agency, then some successful examples exist that can be used as a demonstration to develop cross agency support. However, to even get there, there are four meetings usually needed to get simplification on the agenda.

The first meeting is with the IT group, the operations side. This can be the operations department on the Intel or the mainframe side. Operations has the job of meeting service levels and creating highly available and secure operating infrastructure.

The second conversation is with the application developers. Typically, they are building applications for a particular platform. They are creating stand-alone application environments where a new application is deployed. These environments have everything all together and are supposed to be hosted separately. If the application requires data or operations from another environment, the developers define the boundary or interface that defines how to transfer information between those communities. These application developers have to be brought in so they know that they might develop for one platform and deploy it on another platform, if that's where it will make economic sense. They also need to know the tools, the workflow and how to work with the IT organization to deploy on each platform.

A third meeting must be held with a decision maker — a CIO or business unit executive, a department or agency director — so that they can understand the benefits for operations and the applications developers. The fourth conversation is a joint meeting across the IT operations and applications development communities to decide on a proof of concept scenario. This proof will be to take a business problem developed on one platform and deploy it on another platform to create an active connection between two stovepipes. This creates a working relationship across organizations. Assuming that this project will succeed, the agency can move onto the next simplification project.

Ideally, this proof of concept could be a problem that is blocking a huge investment. For example, take an agency that endured a 10 percent budget cut which they had no idea how to meet. Each team could give a little bit to reach that amount. By collaborating, they could get substantially greater reduction than the target. Moreover, it wouldn't be an artificial reduction but could actually result in a more efficient end-to-end operation.

From a security point of view, the problem is how to identify who accessed an instance of data. Often the problem occurs where there is a portal that is capturing new Web requests and signs on the client. The client then calls an application tier that has some type of service orientation application server that, in turn, calls a database to update, insert or query some kind of information.

The database keeps a log of who accessed what. But did the log register credentials of the organization that requested the data, which in this case would be the intermediate server, or those of the client who originally signed into the infrastructure? In many cases it is the credential of that intermediate server that is logged and the identity of the actual user is not registered. This creates an exposure because the individual that actually accessed or processed a piece of information is unknown. Many people can be looking at the same database but it only takes one person to leak information. With that kind of non-shared security infrastructure, they may not be identified.

One of the technologies to look for is the audit records and governance. Do they provide the granularity down to who actually used information? This means looking beyond each organizational boundary. The goal is to make those kinds of security associations and to put the architecture in place that facilitates that type of authentication or passing of credentials, from one piece of the network to another, along the entire end-to-end workflow.

It would take an entire lifetime for the federal government to perform complete infrastructure simplification throughout all of its various entities. Most agencies are simplifying to some degree, but it's too early to measure their success. Nonetheless, federal managers can start looking at the simplification process now, to see what makes sense and to cherry pick the best methods.

■ ■ ■

Jim Porell is a Distinguished Engineer and Chief Architect for IBM's mainframe software. He chairs the zSeries Software Design council that brings together all IBM technology in the deployment of customer solutions utilizing mainframe technology. Jim led the architecture development for IBM's Multi-Level Security technology for z/OS, including the database server, DB2.

Jim focuses on security and business resilient solutions for customers. He has been consulting to government and commercial customers on secure computing infrastructure for more than 10 years. He also has participated in several government efforts ensuring the protection of critical computing infrastructure. He can be reached at 845-435-6593 or jporell@us.ibm.com.

[8]

THE "SERVICE WAY" TO SECURITY

To enhance security – and simultaneously prevent "stove-piping" of systems – agencies are turning to Service Oriented Architecture (SOA), a collaborative system for linking resources on demand, with a common infrastructure based on open standards. Instead of a heterogeneous mix of systems and applications, each with its supporting database and storage systems, SOA integrates system functions in a way that provides managers with the actionable data they need, when they need it.

> ## "WE WILL EITHER FIND A WAY, OR MAKE ONE."
> — Hannibal (247-183 B.C.), Carthaginian General

by PAUL B. PATRICK

The latest challenge for federal agencies concerns not just the security of their individual computer systems. Today's newest imperatives are data accessibility and collaboration. Managers increasingly feel pressure to cross-link their IT systems with those of other agencies on a daily basis, and to leverage that capability in the event of a terrorist strike or natural disaster. However, the conventional technologies that served agencies and their applications so well in the past are not up to these daunting requirements.

At the same time, federal managers are under the gun to be more agile in addressing changes in opportunities and mission goals. That's why they're embracing a new way: Service Oriented Architecture (SOA). While security and resiliency have long been requirements for the federal government's systems and infrastructure, the need for greater collaboration among agencies is driving a paradigm shift in the way those systems are designed, implemented and managed.

SOA, which is often confused with Web services, is an architectural approach to designing system components as services that focus on a courser grain type of approach, rather than the fine grain focus of the traditional object-oriented programming model. These services can then be combined to create new applications without having to develop a significant amount of new code or duplicating previous solutions.

These services also can be reused and shared among several different applications. In this manner, utilizing SOA provides a means to achieve mission agility and better align the tasks of IT with the missions of the agency, resulting in an ability to react quickly to a target of opportunity or a new situation. SOA also provides new capabilities without undertaking the traditional approach of revamping or building a brand new system from scratch. It bestows the ability to leverage existing IT investments that can result in a lower cost of ownership and reduced operational costs.

The most prevalent incarnation of SOA in government agencies is in the form of Web services, which has resulted in the creation of a distributed, heterogeneous environment. Hence, agencies have encountered security problems inherent in trying to secure an architecture defined by many different moving parts, distributed throughout an enterprise or across enterprise boundaries.

The traditional security approach of building enclaves surrounded by firewalls and putting everything behind them is breaking down, especially as agencies try to morph these applications to handle dynamic ad hoc communities of interest that come together and share information about a particular opportunity. Securing applications that must participate within this kind of fluid community environment creates an entirely new set of problems for service or application security. These problems are compounded by an industry practice of wiring security enforcement logic directly into the business logic, making it necessary to modify the source code to change security policy.

Consequently, agencies are now looking to apply the architectural concepts of SOA, to both the building of new applications and to the approaches used to secure them. This will allow applications to be created to support the participation in a community of interest, not just with U.S. agencies or different branches of the U.S. armed forces, but potentially with coalition partners.

Government managers are assessing how to accomplish this goal and how to bring all the components together in a secure manner. They are now looking at the application of SOA for security, in essence turning security into a service that can be used and leveraged, so that applications can participate in various domains without new wiring or re-implementation of applications.

SECURITY AS AN SOA

Security is typically viewed as a big monolithic quality, similar to a large packaged application. On closer examination, it is apparent that security is actually comprised of different services, each focused on a specific task. For

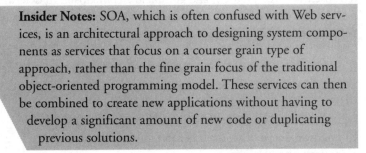

Insider Notes: SOA, which is often confused with Web services, is an architectural approach to designing system components as services that focus on a courser grain type of approach, rather than the fine grain focus of the traditional object-oriented programming model. These services can then be combined to create new applications without having to develop a significant amount of new code or duplicating previous solutions.

SECURITY TECHNOLOGIES THAT ADDRESS THE AUTHENTICATION OF AN IDENTITY ARE DEVELOPED BY A NUMBER OF VENDORS AND USE A VARIETY OF TECHNOLOGIES. THE VARIETY OF AUTHENTICATION TECHNOLOGY HAS INCREASED.

example, authentication is a service that is different and distinct from access control, role entitlement or authorization enforcement. These services are all distinct from the auditing of security decisions made by the aforementioned services.

Auditing also can be a service. Taking security and applying a SOA approach to it is akin to looking at the different kinds of independent functions that make up a security solution, and turning them into services. Following this approach, these functions lose their implementation specific interface and expose their capabilities in a coarse granular manner that hides the details of the specific implementation approach. This allows the specific implementation, behind the security service, to change without affecting the usage of that service.

A notable example is authorization. Many security enforcement systems have an Access Control List (ACL) approach for its authorization scheme. A typical implementation of an ACL based authorization scheme involves accessing code that provides the list of permissions necessary to perform the requested action on the target resource from the authorization system. The authorization system must then determine what permissions the current user has been granted, and complete a comparison to determine if the permissions granted match the necessary set of permissions required to perform the action.

A problem occurs when this same service is utilized as part of a new application, in another government agency where a Role-Based Access Control (RBAC) scheme is used, instead of ACL. In this environment, the business logic containing the code providing the list of permissions required for the comparison does not work. It is too tightly coupled to the ACL implementation of authorization.

In this example, an interface to the authorization service would be built that defines the "is access allowed" service that hides the actual implementation of the underlying authorization system. This allows an application to be built without concern as to whether the authorization service is based on ACL or RBAC. It now becomes a simple question of presenting the identity of the caller, the identifier of the target resource and the intended action attempting to be performed on the resource.

Regardless of the authorization scheme to be used, including permissions, ACLs, RBAC, label, classification or clearances, the actual implementation of authorization service is not visible to the application because it is all hidden behind the service interface. The authorization service can now be implemented in many ways and moved to different types of security implementations, such as ACL based or RBAC based, without fear of changing the implementation.

The flexibility of using a "security as a service" approach can be seen when considering the incorporation of a service utilizing this approach into an application that must support different communities of interest. For example, a new service can be built to participate in an application to support a particular Community of Interest where a simple RBAC scheme is used. Because this service obtains its security enforcement capabilities through a security as a service approach, it can then be easily incorporated into a different application that might have more stringent security enforcement requirements, such as user's clearances and compartments in which they may have been "read in."

THE BUSINESS PERSPECTIVE

From the business point of view, government agencies are attempting to minimize the amount of deployment environment information that a developer needs to incorporate into a business service or application. By accomplishing this, a service can be shared with one or more new environments more freely. This allows them to optimize limited resources, share information more effectively and provide additional agility to address new opportunities or mission objectives.

DATA SNAPSHOT

Is it anticipated that the security mechanisms used in today's applications will meet the future needs for security?

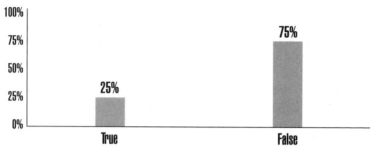

Changes in security technology and requirements will continue to be an issue in the development of applications, as illustrated in the results of the survey.

Download the complete research study for free at www.theblackbooks.com
Source: 2005 Larstan Business Reports

Historically, sharing a particular capability would have entailed taking it to the new environment and changing the code. Avoiding the need to change the code of a business service or application provides critical business agility to create new applications, to more quickly address mission or business opportunities. An additional business benefit is the ability to dynamically adjust the security policy and enforcement mechanisms in near real time.

An example that illustrates the benefits of this capability is that Homeland Security might have information about terrorists that has a security classification that would normally restrict its sharing to a small subset of communities, such as federal law enforcement. However, under a threat of a terrorist attack, Homeland Security will raise the threat level higher, to orange, or even red. Now there is a need to share information that normally would not have been shared, because of a change in context. That context is the threat level that may now be high enough to grant access to additional information to individuals that ordinarily wouldn't have access, such as first responders and local and state law enforcement.

The business context is that Homeland Security can now be more responsive to the situation in sharing sensitive information to a broader community based on the threat level. The net effect is an increase in agility. The agency now can move more quickly and they don't need to change code or redeploy. This can be especially critical in situations where there may be only hours, or minutes, to react.

BRIDGING THE IDENTITY GAP

It is typical for a given agency to have more than one form of security infrastructure in place to protect business services and applications. This situation is a result of changes in technology and changes in security practice. The security technology and practices used to protect applications in the 1970s and 1980s have changed, as the threats against these systems and applications have become more sophisticated.

Some of these security technologies are commercial off-the-shelf (COTS) products from software vendors, and others are internally developed within an agency or by an agency's system integrator. Because of the information assurance requirements of most government applications, COTS products that provide information protection must meet a certain level of government qualifications, such as the NIAP Common Criteria certification, or some other baseline qualification.

Security technologies that address the authentication of an identity are developed by a number of vendors and use a variety of technologies. The variety of authentication technology has increased. This is the result of both changes in authentication mechanisms and in the increase in the number of applications a given user must interact with in the normal course of performing their assignments. As a result, technology such as Web Single Sign-On (SSO) has been introduced to address the issue of forcing the user to authenticate to each application with which they directly interact.

This variety of authentication technology has created a set of new problems associated with building applications that now must interact and share with other applications and services hosted by other federal agencies, and even foreign allies. It is unrealistic to imagine, at this point, that all agencies have the exact same identity security technology. As a result, when the need arises to bring a community of interest together dynamically to respond a brand new opportunity or a potential threat, it is doubtful that all the members of that community will treat identity in the same way.

Consequently, an immediate problem occurs as to how to propagate identity to a different agency and what format that identity should take. Once an identity is brought into an application that is hosted by a member of the community, will that application understand the format of the identity and whether the identity is valid? This is the problem with transforming identity from one format to another without removing trust. To be part of the community, a level of trust must be established.

The Department of Defense is interested in using the Common Access Card (CAC), smart cards that hold digital certificates, to provide a strong form of multi-factor authentication. However, many of the back-end legacy systems being accessed by these cards were built in the 1980s or 1990s and do not understand these identity authentication systems, since they typically use a username/password approach. Because of this disparity in authentication mechanisms used to secure applications, a major problem has become identity transformation. Typically, this problem was handled either by the source code of the business logic that had to handle each of the possible identity formats, or by creating a unique solution that obtained the necessary token formats required by the legacy system. In short, it became a problem that needed to be addressed on an application-by-application basis.

Two key systems concepts are required to address an identity transformation problem:

- The realization that multiple means to authenticate an identity will exist.
- An understanding of whether the sender will be responsible for adapting to the target, or whether the target will adapt to the sender.

The latter is called a "sender makes right" or "receiver makes right" model. Both concepts address the questions of whether an assertion of identity, such as what occurs with digital certificates, or a re-authentication scheme will be required for authentication.

Most legacy applications require a "sender makes right" kind of model. In this model, the application or business service needs a means to acquire the appropriate set of credentials to re-authenticate with the legacy application, based on the current user's identity. Rather than continuing the practice of each application or business service addressing this problem individually, the security as a service approach provides credential exchange services through which an application can obtain the necessary credentials in the appropriate format for the target system. This approach has the additional benefit in that it can manage the mapping of identity credentials from a central location or by individual users, reducing the overall cost of managing the solution.

As new applications and services are constructed, they often provide the ability to support multiple forms of identity propagation. This is usually based on emerging industry standards, such as Kerberos, SAML, etc. These new identity forms often come in the manner of assertions, and thus follow the "receiver makes right" model. The primary goal of this approach is to allow the application or business service to participate in a number of different communities, each of which may have defined its own approach to identity propagation, while limiting the impact of the developer of the business logic. Associated with this approach is the strong need for trust.

In an assertion model, it is critical for a trust relationship to be established between the receivers of the assertion, known as the "relying party", and the issuer of the assertion, known as the "authority," who is vouching for

Insider Notes: Taking security and applying a SOA approach to it is akin to looking at the different kinds of independent functions that make up a security solution and turning them into services. Following this approach, these functions lose their implementation specific interface and expose their capabilities in a coarse granular manner that hides the details of the specific implementation approach.

the validity of the identity being asserted. Here, the security as a service approach provides an "identity assertion" service that is capable of consuming and validating the various forms of identity tokens, thereby eliminating this situation from being handled by the business logic itself. This model has the additional benefit of not requiring every identity that might use an application to have and maintain an account. Concepts such as right, privileges and other types of attributes can usually be contained in the assertion, reducing the amount of administration that is required. This is very similar to the use of the Common Access Card that can also contain information about the holder of the card.

NOT UP TO GRADE

Many of the classic approaches to information security no longer are sufficient to address the security requirements of new systems being built today. Control of access to information through the use of authorization is a good illustration of one such approach that needs modernizing. Authorization is the typical security mechanism used to control whether a user can perform a specific action on a target resource. Consequently, when trying to perform an action, the first thing the authorization system must determine is whether the user is permitted to perform this action. If that action is to retrieve some information, this check only determines if the user has the ability to perform the action.

It begs the question: what are the security consequences when the action is to perform a query for information? Typically, security systems used to protect access assume that whatever information comes back from the query, the user is permitted to see. The problem that many agencies face is that it is the information itself, not the ability to make the query, that needs to be controlled. That's because the information itself has been classified to restrict access to individuals at particular security levels. Therefore, controlling the ability to make the query is no longer sufficient.

There is a need to start looking at the information coming back from the query and applying authorization to the elements of the information itself to control whether the user is able to obtain that information in part or in whole. When it is deemed that the user can obtain only certain parts of the information, a technique called "redaction" can be used to remove information that the caller is not permitted to see.

This removal process can be accomplished using a couple of different techniques. For example, it can be done with the equivalent of an electronic black pen, where elements not to be seen are encrypted and the encryption key is not handed out. In this manner, the particular elements could be altered to remove sensitive information, or the element could be physically removed. However, there's a problem. Physical removal depends on how the information is structured; it could change the integrity or structure of the information as a whole. Removal must be handled with care.

Regardless of the technique, the information coming back must be reviewed prior to delivering it to the user, to remove anything that the user is not authorized to see. This is not as much of an issue in captive communities, where all information is available to all members of the community. Nor may it be a problem if the facility that stores the information enforces a similar type of check. However, this is not always the case and a solution still needs to be provided.

Considering the business problem of dynamic communities that have joined together and are trying to share information, how can specific information be stripped out for community members who have a more restricted access, such as local and state law enforcement, and still provide them information that is critical? This is where an additional check needs to be done on the information being returned.

The dilemma is compounded by the fact that not all information is in an information system, such as a database or packaged application, which can perform this level of filtering or redaction scheme by itself. Because the information is stored in so many forms and in so many different storage schemes, all with very different types of security mechanisms, there is a need for a uniform, consistent way of filtering the information without necessarily having to relocate information to a single store, or worse yet, develop code in the business service that provides this level of enforcement.

Moreover, it is not realistic to expect that every application will provide the necessary redaction scheme, or that there will be some form of information access gateway or proxy that enforces redaction policies. It is especially critical that the redaction enforcement scheme is not hardwired to a particular security approach, so that as context, government policy and requirements change, the level of service can also be dynamically changed to meet current needs.

SECURITY AS A SERVICE

The problem here is not that the various programs or projects being built to generate capabilities for the government don't have security. The problem is that every one of them has their own type of security. As a result, agencies are faced with a sea of various independent pieces of security functionality, many of which are either baked into applications or are custom built. With that in mind, as the government tries to migrate into this new world of sharing information, the need to start building these new applications that interface with the existing applications and do not contain embedded security enforcement logic increases in importance.

At the same time, these agencies are faced with the fact that the Office of Management and Budget (OMB) has not increased their budgets to allow them to dispose of everything they have purchased in the past and start all over again, especially in security. Agencies now find themselves facing the familiar problem of how to do more with existing systems. With regards to security, the problem becomes how to leverage existing security investments, both those that are locked up in an application and those that are stand-alone products, in new ways that allow the creation of a new generation of services and components to meet the changing requirements of government.

In addition, because of the new mandate to share, agencies must consider how to build bridges between all of these islands of security to allow interoperability while keeping administrative overhead to a minimum. Many of these islands of security were implemented back when the world consisted of a small number of analysts sitting at a portal. Suddenly, the world has morphed into much larger communities of users, where membership is dynamic.

With this increasing demand for sharing and collaboration, the question arises as to how to take security, and turn it into a service, similar to any other business service, so it can be leveraged from a number of different applications distributed throughout an agency, the country or, perhaps, the entire world. One approach attempted was to mimic the Web services paradigm and wrap islands of security, similar to how any legacy application can be wrapped, as Web services. This would allow these "security services" to be invoked anytime a security operation was needed.

However, this approach has some downsides. First, the security enforcement is remote. While remoteness provides a level of separation good for isolation purposes, it does mean that the communication has to be secured between the requestor of the security server and the security system providing the service. So how does a secure remote request for a security decision occur? This demands complex actions that would be placed back on the developer of the business logic. The second potential issue is with performance. With the security enforcement point remote, there is the additional overhead of binding to the network, transmitting the request and obtaining the response.

The performance impact can be substantial. For example, an authorization service was put up in a particular program that could be accessed remotely as needed to make a decision. What was found was that the performance of the remote system was unacceptable because it was too slow. When the decision point was moved nearer to the entity being protected, it resulted in a greater than 70% performance increase. Third, if decisions need context information, such as argument values for a business request, this requirement must be passed to the remote security service. Providing this information not only can impact performance but also expose potential sensitive data inappropriately. The key is to enhance security, without hindering performance. For some agencies, this task amounts to a Catch-22.

Insider Notes: From the business point of view, government agencies are attempting to minimize the amount of deployment environment information that a developer needs to incorporate into a business service or application. By accomplishing this, a service can be shared with one or more new environments more freely. This allows them to optimize limited resources, share information more effectively and provide additional agility to address new opportunities or mission objectives.

There are other inherent problems with a remote security service implementation, such as remote security service failure. If there are many different applications or business services all relying upon a remote security service, should that security service goes down, it could take a single application, the entire agency or even more down with it. A catastrophic failure could result not only because of a hardware or software problem with the remote security service, but it could also make anything that depends upon this remote service more vulnerable to a denial of service attack. This could occur simply by overloading the remote security service, by placing upon it an extreme application load on business services that depend upon the security service.

This situation creates a concern about isolation. Since security is about risk mitigation, while attempting to leverage this security service, risk may have been increased because it created a single point of failure. Of course, good practice requires that more than a single instance of a security service be available, but that could introduce even more complexity into the business logic that makes use of a security service, such as requiring developers to handle retry attempts and failover to other security service instances.

Regardless of whether the implementation of a security service is local or remote, it is critical that the service designer think about multiple, different implementations of the service. It is a common mistake to overlook this issue when designing services. Maybe it's an ACL scheme today, a role scheme tomorrow, and three weeks later it's a label scheme. The problem isn't that the government changes its mind that quickly, but that this service may need to be deployed in a number of different places, each of which has its own different security scheme.

The design of security services is critical, because it needs to effectively hide or abstract the details of the various possible security implementations away from application developers. In addition, the design should incorporate mechanisms to allow additional information, such as context, to be provided. Finally, the design should hide whether the actual implementation is either remote from the calling business logic or local to it. One of the most critical issues here is that sensitive information on which decisions are based, such as identity, must be provided in a format that allows for validation against tampering and authenticity.

Although several existing applications used by agencies are written to either contain the security enforcement logic within the business logic or to call a security package or service, a number of agencies have been turning to container-based environments, such as J2EE. Interest in container-based environments is growing, because they abstract much of the infrastructure away from the developer. Containers fundamentally change the way a number of critical aspects, such as transactions and communications protocols as well as security can be integrated, so that the application or business service developer no longer needs to handle them directly.

The good news is that many of the popular container-based environments feature inter-positioning points where security as a service capabilities can be integrated, thus removing the need for the business logic to contain calls to security functionality. These interception points typically provide a place in the middle of the invocation path where one could place security enforcement. These interception points come in different shapes and sizes, depending upon the container type and vendor. As such, there are a couple of techniques that could be used to achieve this integration.

SECURITY SERVICE INFRASTRUCTURE

If one can get past the confusion around "security as a service," meaning to make all security functionality available as a Web service, and understand the impact of local and remote implementations, it becomes clear that there is a lot more to providing this concept than just exposing the functionality.

Insider Notes: Consequently, an immediate problem occurs as to how to propagate identity to a different agency and what format that identity should take. Once an identity is brought into an application that is hosted by a member of the community, will that application understand the format of the identity and whether the identity is valid? This is the problem with transforming identity from one format to another without removing trust. To be part of the community, a level of trust must be established.

DATA SNAPSHOT

Do the applications you control or develop incorporate security enforcement logic within the business logic directly?

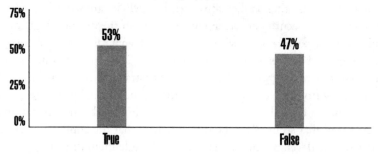

The perpetuation of the practice to embed security enforcement logic directly into application business logic will continue to result in increased cost of maintenance and delays in adapting to changing security requirements.

Download the complete research study for free at www.theblackbooks.com
Source: 2005 Larstan Business Reports

The reality is that there needs to be a consistent interface to each of the security services that hides the actual implementation and its location, provides auditing of each security decision and incorporates management.

To address these needs, it is important to create an infrastructure layer between the business logic or container and the implementation of the service. This infrastructure layer has to be designed in such a way that it hides whether or not the implementation of the service is remote or local, as well as be extensible so that the service implementation can be swapped out and something else swapped in without having to make changes to the code. This is critical when moving applications or business services and designing them to be deployed in a number of different environments.

Additionally, it is important to think about the Information Assurance (IA) requirements that may be placed on an application or business service. These can differ from environment to environment. As such, one of the key services in a security infrastructure is auditing; its placement in the infrastructure also is critical. Rather than requiring business logic calling the security infrastructure to perform the appropriate level of auditing, or requiring security service implementations to do the same, a framework at the heart of this infrastructure, which mediates between the security service request and the security service implementation, will provide the ideal place to report both attempts and results of all security decisions.

Since the framework acts as a mediator between service interface and service implementation, it has access to all the information passed between the two and can provide this same information to the audit service. This, alone, can be a significant gain in agility, especially when proposed systems must undergo IA testing before being fielded or placed in operation. Finally, the use of a framework within a security service infrastructure helps ensure loose coupling, allowing for evolution and support of new standards that continue to emerge.

THE ROLE OF STANDARDS

The various standards communities, such as W3C, OASIS and others, have been primarily focused on protocols and syntax representations for Web services. At the time of this writing, the current state of standards in the area of security for Web services is that there is one standard issued, and a number of specifications attempting to be standardized. In addition, almost all of the work being done to date has been focused on the transmission and establishment of identity between two points.

Efforts to create standard formats and protocols for the exchange of identity are key to the success of an SOA approach to address the sharing of information. Standards such as SAML provide an ability to exchange identity information, convey an indication of the authority which is vouching

Insider Notes: The problem that many agencies face is that it is the information itself, not the ability to make the query, that needs to be controlled. That's because the information itself has been classified to restrict access to individuals at particular security levels. Therefore, controlling the ability to make the query is no longer sufficient.

THE HORIZONTAL FUSION PROGRAM

The Horizontal Fusion Program was created by the U.S. Department of Defense, to provide a "test bed" for the development of a Net-Centric environment and SOA. In 2004, this program entered its Quantum Leap-2 phase. A central task of Quantum Leap-2 was to demonstrate secure cross-domain exchange of information between U.S. and coalition forces.

To create a more realistic scenario, this testing simulated coalition forces and participants from U.S. forces distributed throughout the country. In accordance with Net-Centric Enterprise Services (NCES), Horizontal Fusion utilized a set of core security services to provide a uniform approach to security throughout the scenario. The Horizontal Fusion FY2004 After Action Report stated: "The implementation of the security services was perhaps the most challenging part of the FY2004 Horizontal Fusion effort."

An important security observation regarded the impact of the geographic distribution of the security services themselves. Throughout Quantum Leap-2, Horizontal Fusion experimented with the placement of security services at various locations. In one configuration, the Classification Policy Decision service (CPDS) was located at a command in the Pacific, while the other security services were located on the east coast. Within this configuration, it was determined that the latency introduced by the distance between the service's consumers, the Mars Portal and back-end services and the service itself, was unacceptable. As a result, the CPDS was moved and co-located with the other security services. This change in location boosted performance almost 70%. Although additional bandwidth would have the potential to mitigate some of the latency concerns, the report goes on to provide guidance that consideration for bandwidth and distribution must be carefully thought out when deploying an operational environment.

The After Action Report also pointed out that highly utilized core services, such as security, could become a bottleneck in an operational enterprise. It recommended the use of a federation across a number of these types of services as an approach to improve performance. Federation would also help to address the concern that failure of a single instance of a critical service would cripple the entire enterprise.

The Horizontal Fusion Program also needed to label all information, whether in motion or at rest, with a metadata tag indicating the classification of all data, to meet the Information Assurance (IA) target. This was required to enforce policies that governed an individual's ability to access information with certain classifications. The program identified a number of the legacy data sources that did not support, nor provide provisions to support, the labeling of data. Therefore, each legacy data source or service would need to develop an incremental solution, to support the needs of the larger community. Because of the vastly different types of information and manners in which they were stored, it was deemed unrealistic to follow a singular approach.

The requirement to label information also identified that information and services access control, based solely on role and clearance, was typically insufficient to meet the needs of an integrated, networked force. Additional attributes, such as rank, operational component and location, would be needed to support concerns with data aggregation and privacy rights. Because the definition of access control requirements evolved throughout the cycle, coding requirements continued to change. The report indicates that it expects the authorization scheme to continue to evolve and that a phased approach, which supports a hybrid environment of legacy and new schemes, will be critical to the success of any solution.

A final observation was that without federation, it would not be possible for this type of environment to meet the security requirements of a Net-Centric environment. The existence of multiple security services, each under different administrative control and utilizing different back-end stores, requires synchronization. It is an imperative that individual operational areas retain control over their information and access control policies. The report further suggests that the lack of support for federation that can enable both global and local policy decisions, places an increased burden on administration and can lead to solutions that create a single point of failure in each operationally deployed area.

for that identity which can be verified, and potentially propagate attributes about the identity between parties. These features can help reduce the administrative overhead associated with the management of identity in an environment consisting of multiple authentication schemes and multiple identity systems. Coupled with standards such as XML, Digital Signature, XML Encryption, WS-Security, SAML and other identity token formats, identity can now be safely and securely exchanged between parties. But exchange of identity is only a small part of overall security.

The problem, which is not unique to the government, is that while the specification of a standards-based approach to establish and propagate identity is critical, the protection of access to information and the reporting of attempts to access are also important. Since many of the government's prominent systems are doing queries that yield sensitive information, they need to be protected at a lower level and with support for finer granularity. Standards such as XACML, which define syntax that describes authorization policy with fine grain support, are beginning to be adopted. This standard provides the ability to finally have a common vocabulary among various authorization engines that will enable the ability to manage authorization policy in a vendor neutral manner, and also be applied to different implementations. It's advances like this that are critical to address the management headaches that occur in environments where different security enforcement technologies exist.

THE PERILS OF DE-PERIMETERIZATION

As new applications composed of business services from various agencies are created, agencies face another obstacle. In many systems, security of an application is defined by the creation of a hardened network perimeter targeted to keep outside security threats from reaching internal applications. However, as an agency moves into an environment of sharing with agencies not always at the same level of security, this perimeter begins to break down. This is never more evident than in environments, such as the intelligence community, where information, critical to prevent a terrorist attack, now needs to be shared with others outside of that community.

Conventional systems have no way to determine the security of connecting peripheral devices. In today's heightened security environment, that is not sufficient. Indeed, one of the greatest IT security vulnerabilities today comes from mobile workers in the field who require real-time data to make quick decisions. Remote access security must be enhanced, but without sacrificing capabilities. Mobile access, collaboration and continuity of operations in the federal government must be facilitated, but in a secure manner that prevents security breaches.

One of the biggest limitations with a perimeter-only approach is that once anyone gets past the perimeter and inside, the whole world opens up. In this approach, the sharing of information typically involved someone reviewing information, sanitizing the information so that it can be consumed by someone with a lower clearance level, and then publishing this "declassified" information. This required a series of replications. The major problem with replication is that the information gets stale. There is also the potential issue with "data pedigree," the concept that the authenticity or integrity of the information is somehow reduced during this process.

Whether in the government or the commercial world, the dirty little secret is that no one wants to admit the potential for insider threats. Safeguards that are put into place to ensure that people, even those within the organization, only get to see what they have a need to see and nothing more, and then provide a record of what information is accessed, is just good risk management practice. However, sometimes access to information needs to be controlled not just by its classification, but also by someone's "need to know."

One technique used by several agencies is "compartmentalization." With this technique, sensitive information is restricted by both classification and by compartment, limiting access to those at a certain classification level and with access to the compartment. Labeling of the information is the

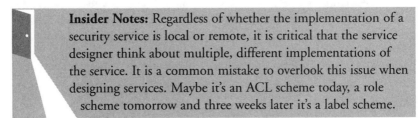

Insider Notes: Regardless of whether the implementation of a security service is local or remote, it is critical that the service designer think about multiple, different implementations of the service. It is a common mistake to overlook this issue when designing services. Maybe it's an ACL scheme today, a role scheme tomorrow and three weeks later it's a label scheme.

most common approach used to implement this technique. But most of the authorization systems, especially the available COTS products, are not enabled to handle this type of security control. When the authorization service is not label enabled, a user may be allowed to make the request, and the information comes back unfiltered. Therefore, to ensure nobody gets access to information that they are not permitted to see, somebody has to filter the information based on the labels associated with it. Often this job falls to an application developer to build a gateway or proxy that sits between the application and the information system, to act as a filter.

An example of this situation is when a user interacts with a portal that contains a portlet that goes directly against an information source to look up terrorist information. If the portlet makes a JDBC call to a database, how is the information being filtered? Some commercial databases provide optional functionality that is capable of providing the appropriate level of filtering, if the caller's identity is provided. Unfortunately, sensitive information isn't always in one of these systems and often the identity of the caller isn't provided. The problem is that the developer of the portlet must know whether there is a database behind that JDBC call which provides the necessary data filtering, or whether the business logic needs to be written to enforce this filtering semantics, itself. It also must be determined how to obtain the appropriate set of credentials, to properly propagate the identity of the caller to the information system being accessed.

In response, a number of agencies are now moving to a model where all information access is through a service interface that hides the actual implementation. The service acts as an intermediary, creating an ideal loca-

Insider Notes: If one can get past the confusion around "security as a service," meaning to make all security functionality available as a Web service, and understand the impact of local and remote implementations, it becomes clear that there is a lot more to providing this concept than just exposing the functionality. The reality is that there needs to be a consistent interface to each of the security services that hides the actual implementation and its location, provides auditing of each security decision and incorporates management.

tion to place the necessary enforcement of information filtering, identity propagation and transaction auditing.

NEW POLICIES, NEW ATTITUDES

Security is by no means just about technology. For many years, it has been viewed mainly as a black and white function. However, recent events have underscored the notion that security involves levels of risk mitigation. Even more critical is the growing cognizance that sharing information is vital to the protection of the country.

The events of 9/11 clearly identified the need to share information, and to do so with more agility. Easier collaboration with other systems must be combined with a greater ability to adapt to policy changes. These interrelated trends will continue to drive the adoption of a more dynamic approach to security policy. It's a difficult task — and it's where SOA starts to affect security. Many agencies continue to operate legacy systems and will not be able to discard them to bring in more flexible systems. Agencies must take these legacy systems and re-purpose them toward goals for which these systems weren't necessarily designed. SOA provides the flexibility to tailor legacy systems to the exigencies of a more fluid environment, without causing disruption to existing applications.

Many government systems are several decades old; antiquated IT methodologies run deep. The attacks of 9/11 provided a wake up call, shouting loud and clear that the entrenched habits of governmental data sharing can't continue unchanged. Although technological limitations contributed to the inability to prevent 9/11, much of the problem stemmed from the hidebound culture of the government bureaucracy. This resistance to change arguably constitutes one of the biggest security hurdles today. A holistic picture must be adopted. After all, the only system that is truly 100% secure is one that is disabled, disconnected, turned off and unplugged from the network. Realistically, such a system is useless. Agencies now must consider deploying security systems that are predicated on potential attacks, while simultaneously calibrating these systems to rapidly evolving environments. That's a tough balancing act.

Transforming security into a service allows the connection of disparate applications, and their adaptation to the security requirements of the respective communities they serve. This adaptability shortens the time it typically takes to create a new application or provide new capabilities, making government more agile. Requirements call for not only making systems secure and recoverable in a disaster, but also for the ability to quickly access information across organizations.

The key security factor that sets today's federal government IT strategies apart from pre-9/11 decisions is the collaborative requirements that are cropping up among agencies. Mandates for greater collaboration are proliferating — and not just within those agencies that are conducting homeland security initiatives. The right information, delivered at lightning speed to the right people, is required to cope with an uncertain world.

One thing is certain: significant strategic benefits can be gleaned if organizations approach security as something more than just an "insurance" policy. Data agility must play a significant role, and a proven way to marry security with agility is the "security as a service" approach.

■ ■ ■

Paul B. Patrick is vice president and chief architect, AquaLogic, BEA Systems, Inc. Prior to this position, he served as chief security architect for BEA, where his responsibilities included driving the security strategy and leading the design of BEA's enterprise security infrastructure product offering. Patrick has over 20 years experience in the high technology industry, with roles in software and hardware development, including network device firmware and diagnostics, network protocols, distributed computing technology, tool development, quality assurance and technical support.

Prior to joining BEA, Patrick worked at Digital Equipment Corporation for 13 years, where his responsibilities included serving as technical leader for the development of distributed object technology, including Digital's ObjectBrokerT CORBA product and technology to bridge the COM/OLE and CORBA object models. He also is the author of several patent applications in the areas of security and service-based architectures. He can be reached at Patrick@bea.com.

GLOSSARY

ACL	Access Control List
APEC	Asia Pacific Economic Cooperation
ATM	Automated Teller Management
CAC	Common Access Card
CAEIAE	Centers of Academic Excellence in Information Assurance Education Program
CCS	Computer Company Services
CIP	Capital Improvement Plans
CI/KR	Critical Infrastructure and Key Resource
CIO	Chief Information Officer
CIS	Center for Internet Security
C-IV	Consortium of California Counties (Merced, Riverside, San Dernardino and Stanislaw)
CME	Common Malware Enumeration
COE	Common Operating Environment
CONOP	Federal Concept of Operations
COTS	Commercial off the Shelf
CPDS	Classification Policy Decision service
CRM	Customer Relationship Management
CSD	Computer Security Division
CSIRT	Computer Security Incident Response Teams
DCID	Department of Central Intelligence Directive
DHS	Department of Homeland Security
DISA	Defense Information Systems Agency
DOD	Department of Defense
DOE	Department of Energy
DOJ	Department of Justice
EFT	Electronic Funds Transfer
EOP	Executive Office of the President
ERP	Enterprise Resource Planning (ERP)

ESF	Emergency Support Functions
EU	European Union
FBI	Federal Bureau of Investigation
FEA	Federal Enterprise Architecture
FIM	Federated Identity Management
FIPS	Federal Information Processing Standards
FISMA	Federal Information Security Management Act
FTC	Federal Trade Commission
FTP	File Transfer Protocol
GAO	Government Accounting Office
G2B	Government to Business (G2B)
G2C	Government to Citizen (G2C)
G2E	Government to Employee (G2E)
G2G	Government to Government
GPE	Government Paper Elimination
HR	Human Resources
HSOC	Homeland Security Operations Center
HSPD	Homeland Security Presidential Directive
IA	Information Assurance
IAM	Information Access and Management
IDP	Identity Provider
IDS	Intrusion Detection Systems
IDWG	Internet Disruption Working Group
IETF	Internet Engineering Task Force
IIMG	Inter-agency Incident Management Group
INCITS	International Committee for Information Technology Standards
IRS	Internal Revenue Service
ISP	Internet Service Providers
ISS	Information Systems Security
IT	Information Technology
IWWN	International Watch and Warning Network

J2EE	Java 2 Platform Enterprise Edition
JDBC	Java Database Connectivity
LAN	Local Area Network
MS-ISAC	Multi-State Information Sharing and Analysis Center
NIAP	National Information Assurance Partnership
NCES	Net-Centric Enterprise Services
NCRCG	National Cyber Response Coordination Group
NCSA	National Cyber Security Alliance
NCSD	National Cyber Security Division
NFS	Network File System
NGN	Next Generation Network
NIPP	National Infrastructure Protection Plan
NIST	National Institute of Standards and Technology
NRP	National Response Plans
NSA	National Security Agency
NSF	National Science Foundation
NSTISP	National Security Telecommunications and Information Security Policy
OAS	Organization of American States
OASIS	Organization for the Advancement of Structured Information Standards
ODBC	Open Database Connectivity
ODOO	Observe, Decide, Operationalize and Optimize
OECD	Organization of Economic Cooperation and Development
OLAP	Online Analytical Processing
OMB	Office of Management and Budget
PDA	Personal Digital Assistants
PKI	Public Key Infrastructure
POS	Point of Sale
PSTN	Public Switched Telephone Network

RBAC	Role-Based Access Control
RF	Radio Frequency
RISC	Reduced Instruction Set Computing
ROI	Return on Investment
RS	Records Services
SAML	Security Assertion Markup Language
SAN	Storage Area Network System
SCM	Supply Chain Management
SCSI	Small Computer Services Interface
SNA	System Network Architecture
SOA	Service Oriented Architecture
SOP	Standard Operating Procedure
SP	Service Provider
SPML	Service Provisioning Markup Language
SSL	Secure Sockets Layer
SSO	Single Sign On
SSP	Sector Specific Plan
TCP/IP	Transmission Control Protocol/Internet Protocol
US-CERT	U.S. Computer Emergency Readiness Team
VoIP	Voice over Internet Protocol
VPS	Victim Protection System
WAN	Wide Area Network
WiFi	Wireless Fidelity
WSDM	Web Services Distributed Management
W3C	World Wide Web Consortium
XACML	Extensible Access Control Markup Language
XML	Extensible Markup Language

SECURITY RESOURCE APPENDIX

Organizations, Companies & Products That Will Help Keep Your IT Infrastructure Safe

Company Name:	Accenture
Address:	11951 Freedom Drive
City:	Reston
State:	Virginia
Zip:	20190
Phone:	312-737-8842
web site:	www.accenture.com

DESCRIPTION

Accenture is a global management consulting, technology services and out-sourcing company. Committed to delivering innovation, Accenture collaborates with its clients to help them become high-performance businesses and governments. With deep industry and business process expertise, broad global resources and a proven track record, Accenture can mobilize the right people, skills and technologies to help clients improve their performance. With more than 126,000 people in 48 countries, the company generated net revenues of US$15.55 billion for the fiscal year ended Aug. 31, 2005.

SERVICES

Accenture has more than 1,100 security professionals helping organizations work through complex security issues such as strategy, compliance, identity and business continuity. Accenture helps organizations deliver increased performance and sustainable cost reductions across the security spectrum. Our Security offerings describe the breadth of solutions that we currently bring to clients.

Securing the Extended Enterprise
- Identity and Access Management
- Secure Web Services
- Secure Data and Rights Management
- Secure Business Application Platforms
- Next Generation Secure Networks
- Secure Mobility

Preventing High-Cost Security Failures
- Security Risk Management and Assessment
- Embedded Business Continuity

Driving Operational Excellence
- Security Strategy and Transformation
- Security Governance and Organization Design
- Effective Privacy and Compliance

Transforming the Security Function
- Security Management Services

Company Name:	BEA Systems, Inc.
Address:	2315 North First Street
City:	San Jose
State:	CA
Zip:	95131
Phone:	408-570-8000, or (US toll free) 800-817-4BEA
web site:	http://www.bea.com/

DESCRIPTION:

BEA Systems, Inc. is a world leader in enterprise infrastructure software, providing standards-based platforms to accelerate the secure flow of information and services. BEA product lines — WebLogic®, Tuxedo® and the new AquaLogic™ family of Service Infrastructure — help customers reduce IT complexity and successfully deploy Service-Oriented Architectures to improve business agility and efficiency.

SERVICES:

BEA Services provide the expert "know-how" in the practical implementation of BEA software across your enterprise. Our Consulting, Education and Support Services are designed to minimize risk and accelerate your return on investment during your entire IT project. BEA Services ensure you have the expertise, knowledge and support you need — from concept to production and beyond.

BEA Services help:
- Mitigate implementation and management risks of enterprise projects
- Accelerate financial returns and increase IT productivity
- Reduce your overall cost of ownership during the entire project, including post-production

For more information, please visit: http://www.bea.com/services/

Company Name:	BMC Software, Inc.
Address:	2101 City West Blvd
City:	Houston
State:	Texas
Zip:	77042
Phone:	+01-713-918-8800
web site:	www.bmc.com/identitymanagement

DESCRIPTION:

Founded in 1980, BMC Software, Inc. [NYSE:BMC] is a leading provider of enterprise management solutions that empower companies to manage their IT infrastructure from a business perspective. BMC Software's Business Service Management (BSM) strategy and, in particular, its Identity Management Solutions, are aligned with business needs to ensure that the challenges of today's IT environments are successfully addressed. With BMC Software, the IT organization manages what matters at a business-service level. A strategic advantage of BSM is the ability to lower the total cost of IT and business operations, comply with regulatory issues and even enhance revenue opportunities. BMC Software enables companies to Activate their Business with the Power of IT.

SERVICES:

BMC Software has collaborated with customers and partners during the past year to build common implementation approaches tied to immediate business needs. BMC Software identified the eight most common implementation approaches that emerged, forming what the company now refers to as Routes to Value™.

Routes to Value provide a clear, competitive differentiator and facilitate customer engagements by simplifying the value of BSM with very clear deployment processes. The Routes to Value are:
• Infrastructure and Application Management
• Service Impact and Event Management
• Service Level Management
• Capacity Management and Provisioning
• Change and Configuration Management
• Asset Management and Discovery
• Incident and Problem Management
• Identity Management

Starting with one or more of these Routes to Value, companies are able to address immediate IT needs while at the same time follow a clear roadmap for full Business Service Management implementation.

FEE:

To take advantage of a BMC Software special offer for readers of Government Security, please visit us at www.bmc.com/identitymanagement/blackbook and enter code bbGS2006.

(estimated value of the offer is $50)

Company Name:	CERT Coordination Center (CERT/CC)
Address:	CERT® Coordination Center
	Software Engineering Institute
	Carnegie Mellon University
City:	Pittsburgh
State:	PA
Zip:	15213-3890
Phone:	412-268-7090
web site:	www.cert.org/nav/index_main.html

DESCRIPTION:

The CERT Coordination Center (CERT/CC) is located at the Software Engineering Institute (SEI), a federally funded research and development center at Carnegie Mellon University in Pittsburgh, Pennsylvania. Following the Morris worm incident, which brought 10 percent of Internet systems to a halt in November 1988, the Defense Advanced Research Projects Agency (DARPA) charged the SEI with setting up a center to coordinate communication among experts during security emergencies and to help prevent future incidents.

While we continue to respond to major security incidents and analyze product vulnerabilities, our role has expanded over the years. Along with the rapid increase in the size of the Internet and its use for critical functions, there have been progressive changes in intruder techniques, increased amounts of damage, increased difficulty of detecting an attack and increased difficulty of catching the attackers. To better manage these changes, the CERT/CC is now part of the larger SEI Networked Systems Survivability Program, whose primary goals are to ensure that appropriate technology and systems management practices are used to resist attacks on networked systems and to limit damage and ensure continuity of critical services in spite of successful attacks, accidents or failures ("survivability").

The CERT/CC is now also part of US-CERT, a joint effort with the Department of Homeland Security's National Cyber Security Division. US-CERT complements and enhances CERT/CC capabilities of preventing cyber attacks, protecting systems and responding to the effects of cyber attacks across the internet.

SERVICES:

Vulnerability Analysis and Incident Response; Survivable Enterprise Management; Education and Training; and Survivable Network Technology

Company Name:	Cisco Systems, Inc.
Address:	170 West Tasman Dr.
City:	San Jose
State:	CA
Zip:	95134
Phone:	408-526-4000
web site:	Cisco.com

DESCRIPTION:

Cisco Systems, Inc. is the worldwide leader in networking for the Internet. Today, networks are an essential part of business, education, government and home communications, and Cisco Internet Protocol-based (IP) networking solutions are the foundation of these networks. Cisco hardware, software and service offerings are used to create Internet solutions that allow individuals, companies and countries to increase productivity, improve customer satisfaction and strengthen competitive advantage. The Cisco name has become synonymous with the Internet, as well as with the productivity improvements that Internet business solutions provide. Our vision is to change the way people work, live, play and learn.

SERVICES:

Cisco provides industry-leading products in the core areas of routing and switching, as well as advanced technologies in areas such as IP telephony, network security, optical and storage networking. In addition to hardware and software products, Cisco provides a broad range of service offerings to its clients, including award-winning technical support and advanced services.

SPECIAL OFFERINGS:

Computer-Based Training: Securing Cisco Routers
Download at http://www.cisco.com/web/about/security/security_services/ciag/workforce_development/securing_cisco_routers.html

White Paper: Continuity of Operation Strategies in the Federal Government
Download at http://www.cisco.com/web/strategy/docs/gov/agencies_secure_resilient.pdf

White Paper: Defense Agencies Meet Readiness Challenges With Commercial Off the Shelf (COTS)-Based Systems
Download at http://www.cisco.com/web/strategy/docs/gov/space_COTS_v2.pdf

FEE:

Complimentary

Company Name:	International Business Machines (IBM) Corporation
Address:	New Orchard Road
City:	Armonk
State:	New York
Zip:	10504
Phone:	914-499-1900
web site:	www.ibm.com

DESCRIPTION:

IBM is the world's largest information technology company, with 80 years of leadership in helping businesses innovate. Drawing on resources from across IBM and key IBM Business Partners, IBM offers a wide range of services, solutions and technologies that enable customers, large and small, to take full advantage of the new era of ebusiness on demand. For more information about IBM, visit http://www.ibm.com. For more information on IBM's on demand strategy, visit http://www.ibm.com/ondemand.

SERVICES:

IBM offers a broad range of security and business recovery products and services, including a multi-level security solution for the IBM eServer zSeries mainframe. Multi-level security solution provides IT administrators with the ability to give users access to information based on their need-to-know, or clearance level, without having to build duplicate infrastructures.

The solution combines IBM DB2 Universal Database to create a virtual secure database that can greatly simplify IT infrastructure by creating a single repository of data to be managed at the row and column level. It is designed to help reduce IT costs, save floor space and administration costs as well as ensure records are more up to date and more easily managed.

The technology also presents opportunities for businesses to develop secure eHosting services off of a single system and database, which is critical as companies continue to evolve virtual environments and create on demand businesses.

Company Name:	Information Systems
	Security Association (ISSA)®
	ISSA Headquarters
	7044 S. 13th Street
	Oak Creek, WI 53154
Phone:	414-908-4949
Toll Free in U.S.:	800-370-ISSA
Fax:	414-768-8001
web site:	www.issa.org

DESCRIPTION:

The Information Systems Security Association (ISSA)® is a not-for-profit, international organization of information security professionals and practitioners. It provides educational forums, publications and peer interaction opportunities that enhance the knowledge, skill and professional growth of its members.

SERVICES:

Member benefits include:

- Professional Networking
- Education
- Conferences
- Webcasts
- Subscription to The ISSA Journal monthly magazine

Company Name:	Infosecurity/Security Leadership Conference Series [jointly produced by (ISC)²® and Infosecurity]
Address:	383 Main Avenue
City:	Norwalk
State:	CT
Zip:	06851
Phone:	203-840-5651
web site:	www.infosecurityevent.com
	www.securityleadershipseries.com

DESCRIPTION:

Infosecurity heightens the sharing of information critical to a more secure and compliant information infrastructure through the delivery of a highly balanced, quality educational program for security professionals, practitioners and business leaders. Infosecurity is committed to advancing the knowledge of emerging threats and vulnerabilities, solutions to mitigate these dangers and best practices in the effort to protect both private and public networks.

SERVICES:

Educational programs, CPE offerings towards CISSPs — courtesy of (ISC)² — new product sourcing, a full spectrum of security products, systems, solutions.

FEE:

$200 off any Infosecurity or Security Leadership Full Conference registration fee of $995.

Company Name:	ISACA®
Address:	3701 Algonquin Road, Suite 1010
City:	Rolling Meadows
State:	Illinois
Zip:	60008
Phone:	847-253-1545
web site:	www.isaca.org

DESCRIPTION:

ISACA is a pace-setting global organization for information governance, control, security and audit professionals. Its IS auditing and IS control standards are followed by practitioners worldwide. It administers the globally recognized Certified Information Systems Auditor (CISA) certification and the new Certified Information Security Manager (CISM™) certification. ISACA publishes a leading technical journal — the Information Systems Control Journal — and it hosts a series of international conferences. Together, ISACA and its affiliated IT Governance Institute lead the information technology control community and serve its practitioners by providing the elements needed by IT professionals in an ever-changing worldwide environment.

SERVICES:

- Membership
- ISACA Bookstore
- Global Conferences and Educational Programs
- K-NET
- Information Systems Control Journal
- Discussion Forums
- Leadership
- Access to Standards, Guidelines and Procedures
- Research
- Certification

Company Name:	(ISC)^2
Address:	33920 US 19 North, Suite 205
City:	Palm Harbor
State:	Florida
Zip:	34684 USA
Phone:	727-785-0189
web site:	www.isc2.org

DESCRIPTION:

Based in Palm Harbor, Florida, USA with offices in London, Hong Kong and Tokyo, the International Information Systems Security Certification Consortium, Inc. (ISC)^2® is the premier organization dedicated to providing information security professionals around the world with the standard for professional certification based on (ISC)^2's CBK®, a compendium of industry "best practices" for information security professionals. Since its inception in 1989, the non-profit organization has certified more than 28,000 information security professionals in 120 countries. (ISC)^2 awards the Certified Information Systems Security Professional (CISSP®) and the Systems Security Certified Practitioner (SSCP®) credentials. The CISSP, the Gold Standard in information security certifications, is the first information technology credential to meet the requirements of ISO/IEC 17024, a global benchmark for certification of personnel. More information about (ISC)^2 is available at www.isc2.org.

SERVICES:

- Maintaining the CBK® for information security (IS)
- Certifying industry professionals and practitioners under an international IS standard
- Providing education
- Administering certification examinations
- Ensuring the continued competence of credential-holders, primarily through continuing education

SPECIAL OFFERINGS:

Get the latest information on trends and issues affecting you — the information security professional. Send your email request for a copy of the (ISC)^2/IDC 2004 Global Information Security Workforce Study to wkfstudy@isc2.org.

Company Name:	The Global CSO Council
Address:	4616 Henry Street
City:	Pittsburgh
State:	PA
Zip:	15213
Phone:	412-268-6755
web site:	www.csocouncil.org

DESCRIPTION:

The Global Council of CSOs is a think tank comprised of a group of influential corporate, government and academic security experts dedicated to raising the awareness of online security issues. The Council encourages dialogue and action to meet the new challenges of online security. The Council focuses on defining the role CSOs should take in corporate, national security and future technology development.

SERVICES:

The Council is the first step in providing senior public and private sector leadership with the following five objectives:

1. Bring together CSOs to address online security challenges in an ever-changing environment, with a focus on business issues rather than technological issues
2. Define the proper role, background and reporting arrangements for CSOs within business organizations
3. Define the role of the CSO in implementing The National Strategy to Secure Cyberspace
4. Determine the appropriate times and means for CSOs to communicate with government on cyber security issues
5. Communicate candidly with technology vendors on a regular basis, to help define security related business needs and offer suggestions on how technology can be used to minimize risks

Carnegie Mellon University's newly formed CyLab, a comprehensive research and education center led by Pradeep K. Khosla and Rich Pethia, will act as the Council's Executive Secretariat. This role supports CyLab's mission of creating a partnership between academia, government and industry-based organizations to create technologies for improving the nation's capabilities in response, prediction, education and development of new technologies for addressing the threats to the cyber infrastructure.

Company Name:	Lucent Technologies
Address:	1100 NY Avenue, Suite 640
City:	Washington
State:	DC
Zip:	20005
Phone:	202-312-5915
web site:	www.lucent.com;
	Government Solutions: www.lucent.com/gov

DESCRIPTION:

Lucent Technologies designs and delivers the systems, services and software that drive next-generation communications networks. Backed by Bell Labs research and development, Lucent uses its strengths in mobility, optical, software, data and voice networking technologies, as well as services, to create new revenue-generating opportunities for its customers, while enabling them to quickly deploy and better manage their networks. Lucent's customer base includes communications service providers, governments and enterprises worldwide. Lucent Technologies is headquartered in Murray Hill, NJ, USA.

SERVICES:

Lucent Technologies has a tradition of excellence in network innovation, technology and leadership for the government. Backed by Bell Labs, Lucent delivers on the promise of ensuring mission-critical, converged communications for the Department of Defense, Homeland Security, civilian and intelligence agencies and their missions. This includes delivering a full-spectrum of security offerings such as Business Continuity and Disaster Recovery, Network Security Assessments, Managed Security Solutions and personalized Security Consulting Services to its government clients. With its four Global Network Operations Centers (GNOC) equipped with Security Operations Centers (SOC), Lucent provides industry leading, real-time security monitoring, management and support of a customer's network on a 24 x 7 x 365 basis. For more information on Lucent's security solutions visit www.lucent.com/security.

Company Name:	## MacLean Risk Partners, LLC
Address:	2506 Penngate Drive
City:	Sherrills Ford
State:	NC
Zip:	28673
Phone:	828-478-3988
web site:	www.macleanriskpatners.com

DESCRIPTION:

In today's fast paced global market, effective security and operational risk management is quickly becoming the differentiator for many businesses. Assuring the trust of your customers, partners and employees is essential to maintaining a competitive edge. Implementing reliable and resilient systems and processes to ensure your enterprise is operational to meet the need of your customers and partners, and can be the difference between being in business, and being out of business. In addition, the current global regulatory environment is driving many organizations to take immediate action to ensure compliance.

SERVICES:

MacLean Risk Partners, LLC works with top fortune global companies, government agencies and consortiums, providing real world practical security and operational risk management consulting for organizations worldwide. We are focused on strategies that align your specific operational risk management needs to your business objectives for cost effective solutions in the following areas:

- Business Continuity and Resiliency
- Information protection for sensitive data including intellectual property and privacy
- Organizational Assessments
- Compliance and Governance Programs
- Vendor and Partner Approaches
- Establishing measurements and metrics to track your company's goals surrounding operational risk
- Electronic Data Discovery

Company Name:	Oracle Corporation
Address:	500 Oracle Parkway
	Redwood Shores, Calif. 94065
	650-506-7000
web site:	http://www.oracle.com

DESCRIPTION:

Oracle's business is information — how to manage it, use it, share it, protect it. For nearly three decades, Oracle Corporation (NASDAQ: ORCL), the world's largest enterprise software company, has provided the software and services that let organizations get the most up-to-date and accurate information from their business systems. Today, Oracle is helping more governments and businesses around the world become information-driven than any other company, by following three principles: simplify, standardize and automate. These principles let companies use high-quality information to collaborate, measure results for continuous improvement, align their stakeholders and communicate a single truth to all their constituents.

SERVICES:

Oracle offers its database, tools and application products, along with related consulting, education and support services to the world's largest and most successful businesses and institutions.

SPECIAL OFFERINGS:

We would like to direct readers to check out www.oracle.com/security, where we offer a plethora of security information that includes white papers, best practices for securing Oracle products, security discussion forums and much more.

FEE:

Priceless.

Company Name: United States Computer Emergency
Readiness Team (US-CERT)

Address: 1110 North Glebe Road
City: Arlington
State: VA
Zip: 22201
Phone: 888-282-0870
web site: www.us-cert.gov/

DESCRIPTION:

US-CERT is a partnership between the Department of Homeland Security
and the public and private sectors. Established to protect the nation's Internet
infrastructure, US-CERT coordinates defense against, and responses to, cyber
attacks across the nation.

Established in September, 2003, US-CERT is a public-private partnership
charged with improving computer security preparedness and response to cyber
attacks in the United States. US-CERT is responsible for analyzing and reducing cyber threats and vulnerabilities, disseminating cyber threat warning information and coordinating incident response activities.

US-CERT also provides a way for citizens, businesses and other institutions to
communicate and coordinate directly with the United States government
about cyber security.

US-CERT is the operational arm of the National Cyber Security Division
(NCSD) at the Department of Homeland Security (DHS). The NCSD was
established by DHS to serve as the federal government's cornerstone for cyber
security coordination and preparedness, including implementation of the
National Strategy to Secure Cyberspace.

SERVICES:

The National Cyber Alert System provides valuable cyber security information
to all users. You can subscribe to free email lists through the US-CERT web
site. The system sends alerts and other cyber security information that provide
guidelines and actions to help you to better secure your portion of cyberspace.
You can receive any or all of the following documents through email:
• **Cyber Security Alerts** — Sign up at www.us-cert.gov/cas
• **Cyber Security Tips** — Sign up at www.us-cert.gov/cas
• **Cyber Security Bulletins** — Sign up at www.us-cert.gov/cas

LARSTAN'S THE BLACK BOOK™ ON
GOVERNMENT
SECURITY

NOTES

LARSTAN's THE BLACK BOOK™ ON
GOVERNMENT
SECURITY

LARSTAN'S THE BLACK BOOK™ ON
GOVERNMENT
SECURITY

LARSTAN's
THE BLACK
BOOK™ ON
GOVERNMENT
SECURITY

Visit www.theblackbooks.com today for more must-read security information.

Also, tell us what you want to see in future editions —
e-mail us at comments@www.theblackbooks.com.

www.theblackbooks.com

LARSTAN'S THE BLACK BOOK™ ON

GOVERNMENT SECURITY

CUTTING-EDGE GUIDANCE FROM THE WORLD'S LEADING EXPERTS

Inside you will discover how to:

» Leverage government buying power to improve software security

» Implement a national cyber security strategy

» Approach identity management in an integrated fashion

» Cut costs while increasing security by simplifying your infrastructure

» Enhance security through a Service Oriented Architecture approach

» Understand how standards improve security

» Work towards true information sharing

LARSTAN
PUBLISHING